Arnold Bennett

Twayne's English Authors Series

Kinley E. Roby, Editor

Northeastern University

TEAS 390

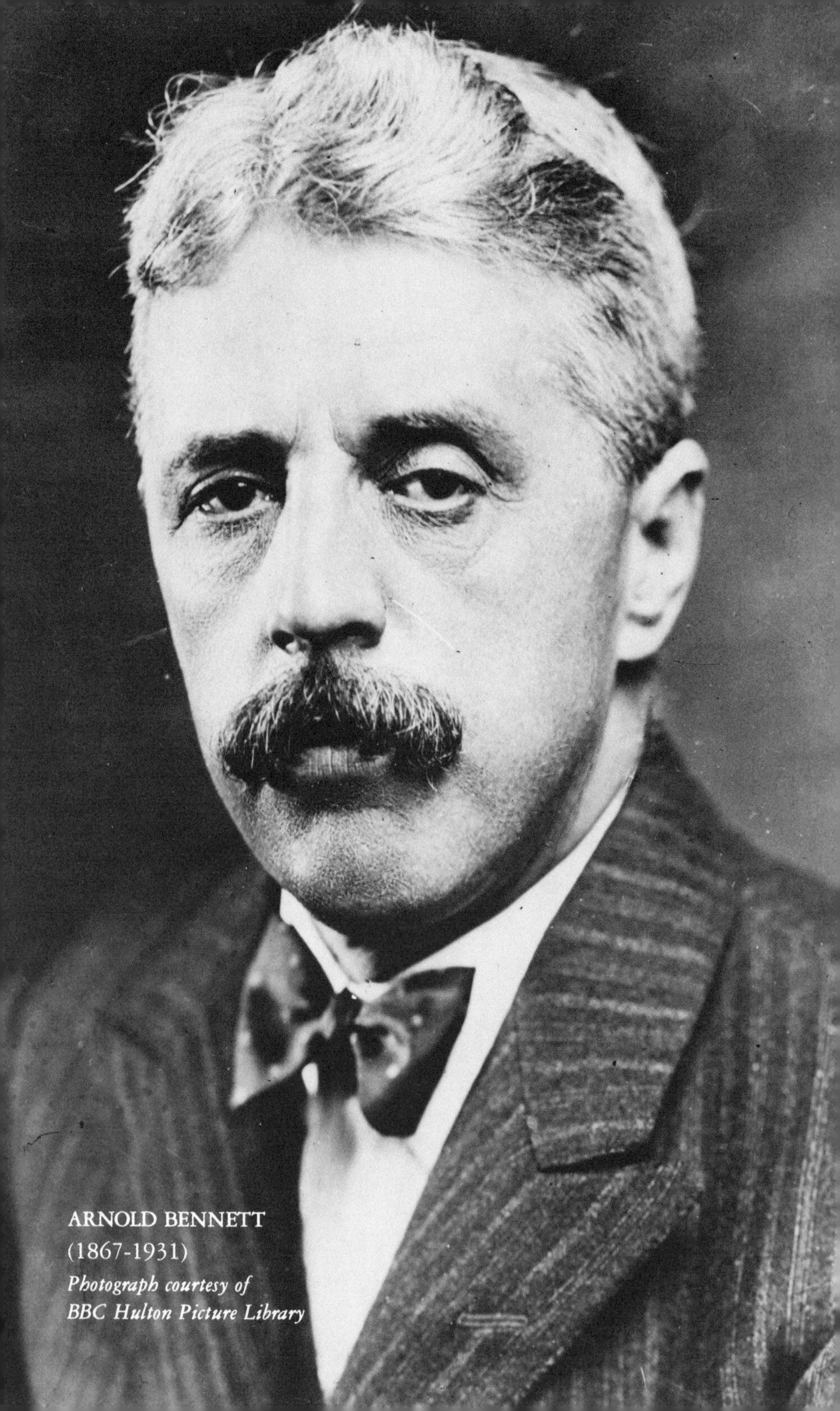

ARNOLD BENNETT
(1867-1931)
Photograph courtesy of
BBC Hulton Picture Library

Arnold Bennett

By Olga R.R. Broomfield

Mount Saint Vincent University

Twayne Publishers • Boston

Arnold Bennett

Olga R.R. Broomfield

Copyright © 1984 by G.K. Hall & Company
All Rights Reserved
Published by Twayne Publishers
A Division of G.K. Hall & Company
70 Lincoln Street
Boston, Massachusetts 02111

Book Production by Marne B. Sultz

Book Design by Barbara Anderson

Printed on permanent/durable acid-free
paper and bound in the United States of
America.

Library of Congress Cataloging in Publication Data

Broomfield, Olga R. R.
Arnold Bennett.

(Twayne's English authors series; TEAS 390)
Bibliography: p. 151
Includes index.
1. Bennett, Arnold, 1867-1931—Criticism and
interpretation. I. Title. II. Series.
PR6003.E6Z64 1984 823'.912 83-18391
ISBN 0-8057-6876-9

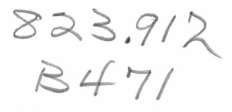
For my Mother
And in memory of my Father

Contents

About the Author

Olga Broomfield is an Associate Professor of English and former Chairperson of the Department of English at Mount Saint Vincent University, Halifax, Nova Scotia. She gives courses on the novel and on Shakespeare and Elizabethan Drama. In developing her master's thesis on the novelist Ford Madox Ford for the Memorial University of Newfoundland, she became interested in the techniques of the Realists and Impressionists at the turn of the nineteenth century. Her work on Ford was commended by Geoffrey Bullough of King's College, University of London. This led to her Ph.D. studies at the University of London under the late critic Geoffrey Tillotson, supported by Rothermere Fellowships. While an active administrator, she maintained a strong interest in writers at the turn of the century, notably Arnold Bennett, a writer she feels has not yet gained all the attention he merits.

Preface

In the development of the English novel one of the recognizable trends is the gradually emerging conception of the novel as Art. Concomitant with the involvement of the novelist in the discovery and perfection of techniques that would permit his representation of life as it appears to the sensitive observer, was his involvement, at the turn of the nineteenth century, in the more frankly psychological approach to the creation of characters and the selection of details for action and scene. Emile Zola's preoccupation with clinically observed surfaces produced *Nana*; Virginia Woolf's preoccupation with studies of states of mind produced *The Waves*; between them, there is Henry James's exquisite structuring of the nuances of *The Portrait of a Lady*. Each of these novels carried its particular experimentation to considerable extremes. And beyond these came James Joyce's sophisticated synthesizing of all the trends in *Ulysses*. Among the pioneers of these works, Arnold Bennett appeared, to all but a few of his critics, as a dated traditionalist preoccupied with superficialities. That he was a highly conscious and knowledgeable artist was frequently lost sight of in the hurly-burly of his business arrangements to gain wealth by wooing the popular taste. Now that Bennett's centenary has passed, it is possible to view more objectively his achievements beside the experiments of his contemporaries and see that Bennett's particular combination of the old and the new enabled him, in his best work, to transcribe carefully the very grain of life, to organize its ordinariness in his unique way, thereby producing profound representations of the irreconcilables of the human situation.

The great mass of Bennett's writing makes it impossible, while the fluctuations in quality make it unnecessary, to consider equally all of his varied productions. In this study, therefore, I concentrate on a discussion of Bennett as novelist, making references to his other work where necessary. In the discussion

ARNOLD BENNETT

of the novels I indicate that he did indeed produce thirty-six,
but I concentrate upon the ten novels possessing greatest
literary merit. My study of his novels is set in the context of his
biography and his views of his art. An understanding of the man
and his craft, although necessarily briefly developed here, is
requisite to an appreciation of his novels.

Olga R. R. Broomfield

Mount Saint Vincent University

Acknowledgments

I wish to thank the Committee on Research and Publications of Mount Saint Vincent University for grants supporting the preparation of the text. I also wish to thank the British Broadcasting Corporation's Hulton Picture Library for the use of their photograph of Bennett as frontispiece. I accord many thanks to Phoebe Smith for her accurate and speedy typing of the text.

Chronology

1867   May 27. Birth, Hanley, Stoke-on-Trent.

1876   Father becomes a solicitor.

1883   Leaves school and enters father's law office.

1885   Passes matriculation for university.

1888   Fails legal examination for second time.

1889   A clerk in the law offices of Le Brasseur and Oakley.

1891   First London publication in *Tit-Bits*—a parody.

1893   Writes the serious story "A Letter Home," published 1895.

1894   Becomes Assistant Editor of *Woman*.

1895   Begins *A Man From the North*, published 1898.

1900   *Polite Farces*, three one-act plays.

1901   J.B. Pinker becomes his agent.

1902   *The Grand Babylon Hotel*. Father dies. *Anna of the Five Towns*.

1903   *The Gates of Wrath*. Moves to France. Published *The Truth About an Author* (anonymously), *How to Become an Author, Leonora*. Conceives idea for *The Old Wives' Tale*.

1904   *A Great Man, Teresa of Watling Street*.

1905   *Tales of the Five Towns, The Loot of Cities, Sacred and Profane Love*

1906   *Hugo, Whom God Hath Joined, The Sinews of War*. *Things That Have Interested Me* (journal extracts) published privately.

1907   Meets and marries Marguerite Soulie. *The Ghost, The Reasonable Life, The Grim Smile of the Five Towns, The City of Pleasure*. Writes play *Cupid and Commonsense* (dramatization of *Anna of the Five Towns*). Begins *The*

Old Wives' Tale. Things Which Have Interested Me, Second Series published privately.

1908   Writes *Buried Alive*. Completes *The Old Wives' Tale*. *Cupid and Commonsense* produced. *The Statue, Buried Alive, How to Live on Twenty-four Hours a Day. Things Which Have Interested Me, Third Series* published privately. Goes to Switzerland for three months.

1909   *What the Public Wants*, produced at the Aldwych. *The Glimpse.*

1910   *Helen with the High Hand, Clayhanger.*

1911   *The Card, Hilda Lessways, The Feast of St. Friend. The Honeymoon* opens at Royalty Theatre. Spends six weeks in America.

1912   *The Matador of the Five Towns. Milestones* begins smashing run at Royalty Theatre. Moves permanently to England. Buys yacht *Velsa. Those United States.*

1913   Moves into Queen Anne home, Comarques, Essex. *The Great Adventure* (dramatization of *Buried Alive*) opens at Kingsway Theatre. *The Regent, The Plain Man and His Wife, Paris Nights.*

1914   *Helen with the High Hand* dramatized. Begins political articles for *Daily News*. Appointed military representative, Thorpe Division Emergency Committee. Mother dies. *The Price of Love and Liberty!* (essays), *From the Log of the Velsa.*

1915   Becomes director of *New Statesman*. Begins tour of Western Front for the government. *The Author's Craft, These Twain, Over There.*

1916   Adopts nephew Richard Bennett. *The Lion's Share, Books and Persons.*

1918   Becomes Director of Propaganda, Ministry of Information. *The Pretty Lady, Self and Self-Management.*

1919   *The Roll Call, Our Women. Judith* opens at Kingsway Theatre.

1920   *The Beggar's Opera* (adapted by Bennett) at Lyric,

Hammersmith. Buys yacht *Marie Marguerite*.

1921 *Things That Have Interested Me*. Formal separation from wife.

1922 Film version of *The Old Wives' Tale*. Meets Dorothy Cheston. *The Love Match* opens at Strand Theatre. *Mr. Prohack, Lilian*. *Body and Soul* opens at Euston Theatre of Varieties. Begins *Riceyman Steps*. Moves to Cadogan Square, London.

1923 *Things That Have Interested Me, Second Series, How to Make the Best of Life, Riceyman Steps, Don Juan*.

1924 *Elsie and the Child*. *London Life* (written with Edward Knoblock) opens at Drury Lane.

1925 *The Bright Island* produced by Stage Society.

1926 Birth of daughter Virginia. *Things That Have Interested Me, Third Series, Lord Raingo*. Begins "Books and Persons" series in the *Evening Standard*. *Riceyman Steps* produced at Ambassadors Theatre.

1927 *The Woman Who Stole Everything, The Strange Vanguard*. Facsimile edition of manuscript of *The Old Wives' Tale*. *Flora* produced in Manchester. *Mr. Prohack* at Court Theatre.

1928 *The Sorrows of Life, Mediterranean Scenes*. *The Return Journey* opens at St. James Theatre.

1929 *Accident, The Religious Interregnum*. *Judith* (opera, music by Eugene Goossens, libretto by Bennett) produced at Covent Garden.

1930 *Journal, 1929*. *Imperial Palace*. Moves to Chilton Court. Begins *Dream of Destiny*.

1931 Contracts typhoid fever in France. Dies March 27.

Chapter One
The Man and His Views

Biography

Arnold Bennett, born May 27, 1867, in Burslem, Staffordshire, the heart of the Potteries, came from generations of potters. He knew they had endured appalling conditions of considerable danger.[1] Such fearful working experiences were not, however, the immediate heritage of his family who considered themselves a rather superior group. The ambition to improve their circumstances is evident in the line as far back as 1786 when Bennett's great-great-grandfather could sign his own name upon the marriage register. His grandfather valued education so highly that when the edict to discontinue teaching writing to poor children in Methodist Sunday Schools came from the Methodist conference, he refused, and with a number of other sympathizers founded, in 1837, the Hill Top Chapel, where he became a trustee and superintendent of an institution that boasted a library.[2]

Enoch, Bennett's father, an intelligent boy who determined to become a professional man, was a master potter at age twenty-two, and could take a partnership in a potting business. When the potting business failed, Enoch was reduced to pawnbroking in the tiny shop where Bennett was born. Upon inheriting his portion of his father's small estate in 1870, Enoch articled himself as a solicitor's clerk and began six years of grinding strain. Indelibly impressed upon young Bennett's memory were his father's dogged struggles which terribly reduced the family's circumstances, but which, by Bennett's teen-age, lifted them into relative affluence. The exciting change was completely symbolized for Bennett in his father's having built a substantial house in a desirable neighborhood which permitted a graciousness of living, an expansion of the spirit, so in contrast to the preceding penurious years, that the novelist never forgot the means of the change.

The family consisted, then, of Enoch, his wife, the former Sarah Ann Longson (of successful farming stock who maintained a prosperous tailoring business in Burslem's central square), and six children, Arnold, Frank, Fanny Gertrude, Emily, Tertia, and Septimus, three other children having died in infancy. Bennett's talent for organization, his interest in sketching, his wish to be abreast of modern trends, culminated in extraordinary projects which he and Frank, marshalling the others, achieved to the joy of their parents and the wonder of their guests. Bennett recalls: "We invented friezes, dadoes, and panels; we cut stencils; and we carried out our bright designs through half a house. It was magnificent, glaring, and immense; it foreshadowed the modern music hall. Visitors were shown through our rooms by parents who tried in vain to hide from us their parental complacency."[3]

High parental expectations pressured the children at all times. For Bennett, his father's expectations took a psychic toll as they are cited as the probable cause of the stammer that afflicted him from infancy. Much speculation about causes has been attached to accounts of Bennett's struggle with this affliction. Margaret Drabble has surveyed the most frequently repeated diagnoses: a childhood fall, his mother's view; a sexual shock in infancy, H.G. Wells's view; and she has drawn her conclusion, with which I agree, that the more likely cause is that "of a child nervous before an over-dominating father with far too high expectations of his children."[4]

Bennett's schooldays are respectable. He began his education at the Infants' Wesleyan School in Swan Square. At ten years of age he entered the Endowed School, in the Wedgewood Institute, Queen Street, Burslem. From that school he moved in 1882 to the superior Newcastle Middle School. In these schools Bennett was at or near the top of his class, became head boy in the Middle School, and played for the football first eleven. He alone in his class in December, 1882 passed the Cambridge Junior Local Examination which qualified him to go on to Newcastle High School and then to university. But his father wanted him to enter his law practice, so, at the age of sixteen, Bennett ended his formal education. He became his father's unpaid clerk who did dull tasks by day and studied for the law by night. He passed the London matriculation examinations, but to his father's disgust and his own great surprise, he failed his law examinations.

Two interests which had developed in school and would have significance in his life were his acquirements of French and

Pitman's shorthand. The latter gave him entry to the world of London as he applied for and secured a job as shorthand clerk with a firm of solicitors that is still operating there. The former helped him establish his first London friendship with a fellow clerk, John Eland, with whom he spoke French, ate at French restaurants, read French newspapers, and with whom he pursued his interest in bookbinding and rare books. This association confirmed what was to be his lifelong interest in France. At twenty-one, then, with borrowed train-fare, he could turn his back on his father's plans for him and set out to follow his own.

For five years Bennett remained with the law firm of Le Brasseur and Oakley. The first two years were lonely for him. Through a friend of his father, Joseph Hill, director of the Blackheath School of Art and also art director at Goldsmith's College, Bennett met in the autumn of 1890 Frederic Marriott, another art teacher who was to become a lifelong friend.[5] Marriott and his wife needed a lodger in Victoria Grove, Chelsea, and invited Bennett to join them. This he did.

In Marriott's circle he found the stimulus to begin seriously to attempt self-education in the arts, particularly in literature. He had to admit that at the age of twenty-one he "had read almost nothing of Scott, Jane Austen, Dickens, Thackeray, the Brontës, and George Eliot,"[6] to name but a few. The following two years did not much change his condition. But he felt driven to write by the expectations of his artistic friends and by a latent desire previously given outlet in mediocre commentary in a hometown newspaper, *The Staffordshire Knot*, founded by his father and a group of friends, and a short story and a serial in the manner of Zola.[7] In 1891 he entered a competition in the popular weekly, *Tit-Bits*, for the best parody of the sensational serial, *What's Bred in the Bone*, written by the popular novelist, Grant Allen. He won the prize of twenty guineas, his parody appeared in a December issue of the magazine, and the Marriotts praised his effort, having earlier assured Bennett that "caricature . . . was a legitimate art form capable of leading to much original beauty."[8]

The article gives evidence of the exuberance on which Bennett was to capitalize later in such novels as *The Card* and *A Great Man*, and in many of his short stories and plays. The parody shows youthful awkwardnesses but is, nevertheless, clever. This success impelled him to further effort so that, in January, 1894, he felt capable of quitting the law to accept an assistant-editorship of a five-year-old penny paper called *Woman* in which his father had been persuaded to invest three hundred pounds.

His feeling of inadequacy stimulated him within the next three years to a sedulous reading of his contemporaries, Henry James, George Moore, Joseph Conrad, among others. He increased his reading of early favorites among the French and Russian novelists and started to range back over his English heritage. Before publishing a single article of worth, however, he began, in 1894, to discuss enthusiastically with George Sturt[9] those techniques he observed in his reading and the tendencies he observed in himself. Gradually, he began to clarify his concept of writing fiction. In October of the same year he wrote to Sturt, who would never compromise his artistic integrity: "I may say that I have no inward assurance that I could ever do anything more than mediocre viewed strictly as art—very mediocre. On the other hand, I have a clear idea that by cultivating that 'lightness of touch' to which you refer, & exercising it upon the topicalities of the hour, I could turn out things which would be read with zest. . . . I would sooner succeed as a caricaturist of passing follies than fail as a producer of 'documents humains'."[10] He was to succeed at both endeavors.

Nevertheless, just before leaving the law for journalism he had written "A Letter Home,"[11] a short story which was published in July, 1895, by *The Yellow Book*, the most avant-garde periodical of the day, the organ of the Impressionists and Symbolists.[12] The story appeared with writings of Kenneth Grahame, Henry James, Edmund Gosse, Walter Sickert, Lawrence Housman, and it received favorable critical attention. It is a cheerless presentation of waste and futility quite artistically achieved. This story marks the first appearance in Bennett's better work of the subject of waste and of the more somber attitudes that were given prominence in Bennett's early serious novels. He restricted his talent for humor in his serious books until the two strains of his temperament were successfully balanced in the creation of *The Old Wives' Tale* (1908).

Early in 1894 Bennett had determined to write a novel. By November, 1895 he complained of his difficulties to Sturt in a letter which indicates the direction of his development. In it he says: "It is the *arrangement* that kills one, the mere arrangement of 'sensation & event'. . . . I feel more sure than ever I did in my life before, that I can *write* in time, & 'make people care', too, as Hy. James says—though praps only a few people."[13]

Within the brief six years of his association with *Woman* Bennett not only established the pattern of his concern about serious writing but also the pattern of frenetic productivity that was to astound and dismay those who came to know him throughout his life. By September, 1900, when he resigned editorship of the magazine, he had, beside his daily work, begun one sensational novel; begun, completed, and published his first serious novel, *A Man From the North*; begun what was to become his first critical success, *Anna of the Five Towns*; had moved from his lodgings with the Marriotts to his first home in Fulham Park Gardens; had published *Journalism for Women;* had written and published three one-act plays called *Polite Farces*; had collaborated on another play with his friend Arthur Hooley, and dramatized with another friend, Eden Philpotts, that writer's novel, *Children of the Mist*. Philpotts, at the time assistant editor of the periodical *Black and White*, wished to gain wealth as well as literary distinction, had already published popular frivolous successes and serious fiction, and had proved to himself that this dual activity was the only reasonable way to achieve his disparate desires. Philpotts's aims and methods were much more appealing to Bennett than Sturt's unheralded aestheticism. Consequently, it was his growing friendship with Eden Philpotts that by 1900 gave Bennett the confidence to pursue popular fiction for financial support and thereby have the means to become a full-time writer who would produce serious writing also.

In the following year he moved to Trinity Hall Farm, Bedfordshire, in part because it was fashionable to live in the country, but more particularly because he wished to ease the final months of his father's decline to death from "softening of the brain." Out of these difficult months Bennett gained the stimulus from his father's reminiscences to create so accurately the Potteries background of *Anna* and, much later, to re-create so movingly the declines and deaths of Darius in *Clayhanger* and of Raingo in *Lord Raingo*. In this year also he saw the necessity of acquiring the services of an agent and secured J. B. Pinker who was to promote Bennett's work with remarkable success.

After his father's death, Bennett's mother returned to Burslem;

his sister Tertia, who had been living with him since her fiancé
accidentally drowned, became engaged to William Kennerley; and
Bennett found himself free and financially able to go abroad to
live. He chose Paris, the city of his early literary interests. At first
he felt lonely and of little consequence. The most apparent
difference in the life swirling around him was the relaxed sexual
freedoms of *la belle époque*. The diffident, woman-shy Northerner
soon acquired a mistress named Chichi who worked as a chorus
girl. Gradually, he became a close friend of Marcel Schwob, a
scholar, critic, and linguist, in whose circle Bennett met French
writers, artists, theatrical people, American and English expatri-
ates. Early in this French period he published anonymously *The
Truth About an Author* (1903), a provocative anti-aesthetic view of
a struggling young writer; *How to Become an Author* (1905), a
helpful manual; *Leonora* (1903), a serious novel of a mature
woman's love affair; and stopped writing for the *Academy* in order
to begin a long series of general essays for *T.P.'s Weekly*. He began
writing much more light, short fiction which was to be collected in
The Loot of Cities (1905) and *Tales of the Five Towns* (1905), and his
first daring novel, *Sacred and Profane Love* (1905), the one novel in
his canon generally repudiated by critics for its vulgarity and lack
of restraint.

Since his twenty-first year and his entry to London, Bennett had
been longing for a love of his own, for marriage and the settled life.
During his first years in Paris this longing had become so compelling that on his thirty-seventh birthday he wrote in his Journal that
he had warned his mother and sister Tertia that he would marry
within the following three years. Within two years he had begun
and ended his disastrous engagement to a young American,
Eleanor Green; within the following year he had more disastrously,
as it turned out, met and married an experienced, older Frenchwo-
man, Marguerite Soulié.

The accounts of Bennett's courtship of Eleanor Green vary,[14]
but it appears that he thought he had established that he was in
love with her, that he had asked her to marry him, and that they
were engaged to be married shortly. He rented a new flat, bought
furniture, sent out invitations, and began receiving wedding gifts.
It also appears that she only flirted with him, tried not to take him
seriously, had little idea of, and less care for, how far he had carried
out his plans, and finally had to break the news to him in a

confrontation in the woods of Fontainebleau which must have been excruciatingly painful to both of them. The scars of this experience he bore to the end of his life. From the great misfortune of his first love affair, he turned to his work and to the comfortable society of married women like his old friends, Mrs. Roy Devereaux, Violet Hunt, and Mrs. Agnes Farley. However, needing secretarial help, through his friends he secured the services of Marguerite Soulié. They were drawn together in conversations that ranged freely over her past experiences and her ambitions, all of which emphasized her possibilities as a congenial companion for Bennett. After a few weekends together, and after a bout of illness during which she nursed him entirely to his satisfaction, Bennett recognized that Marguerite wished their liaison to end in marriage. Not passionately involved, Bennett had some doubts about the union. Nevertheless, six months after meeting her, he married her. She was stylish and clever, a good housewife, and, in the beginning, not too demanding. His circle welcomed her.

Three months after his wedding, in relative comfort and content, he settled himself in his country retreat, Les Sablon, to write the major work he had been considering for four years. Into *The Old Wives' Tale* he poured the wisdom of his maturity. Such was the flow of his artistry that he completed the 200,000-word masterpiece, written in a special calligraphy on special paper,[15] in ten inspired months that included the production of two shorter vivacious, farcical novels, *Helen with the High Hand* and *Buried Alive*, and a bewildering list of essays, short stories, dramatic writings, popular philosophies. The novel won him the respect of many distinguished critics and brought him requests for his work from prestigious literary journals like Ford Madox Ford's *The English Review*. Some months before the publication of *The Old Wives' Tale*, Bennett had begun to write articles headed "Books and Persons"[16] for the *New Age*, another prestigious literary journal with a wide readership. His articles promoting Russian and French writers placed him squarely among the avant-garde. He is credited with being a cultural leader for the aspiring young. At the midpoint of his career he had clearly reached literary eminence.

Throughout these years Bennett had pursued his interest in the theater. After ten years of dramatic publications, in 1909 he was exhilarated by his involvement in the first full-scale production of

What the Public Wants, a play he had written the year before in
Switzerland. It starred Sir Charles Hawtrey and Ben Webster and
drew praise from the discriminating Max Beerbohm.[17] Bennett
immediately wrote *Don Juan de Marana,* a scenario of a play for
Beerbohm's uncle, and *The Honeymoon,* commissioned by Herbert
Trench. The scenario was not developed into a play for five years,
but in 1911 *The Honeymoon,* starring Marie Tempest, was acclaimed
for its humor.

Meanwhile, Bennett was planning *Clayhanger,* a much more
closely biographical novel than *The Old Wives' Tale.* With Marguerite, he revisited the Potteries to refresh his memories. His Journal
record of this visit clearly indicates his intense emotion, and that
intensity in turn permeates the novel. He began writing *Clayhanger* at Brighton, continued it in Switzerland and in Italy, then
finished it in Paris. Traveling with Marguerite and Bennett was
Pauline Smith, a young and talented South African protégée of
Bennett's. He had met her while holidaying at Vevey, recognized
her promise, and swept her along on the tide of his generous
enthusiasm. She is among the earliest of the young writers who
were to benefit from Bennett's unselfish care and one of the few
who appreciated it.[18]

Following the critical success of *Clayhanger* in 1910, Bennett
worked on a stage adaptation of *Buried Alive,* continued to write
articles and book reviews, attended to his voluminous correspondence,[19] moved from Fontainebleau into Paris, and began to
draw together his ideas for *Hilda Lessways,* the second of the
Clayhanger novels. Before he completed and published that novel,
he published *The Card,* later made into a movie starring Alec
Guiness, and with Edward Knoblock wrote the play, *Milestones,*
not to be produced until 1912, but then running for a smashing six
hundred performances.

The always restless Bennett, from his constant trips back to
England, or to favored places on the Continent, finally responded
to requests from his American publisher, George Doran, and went
to the New World. He sailed on October 7, 1911, visiting New
York, Washington, Chicago, Indianapolis, Philadelphia, Boston,
and the universities of the New England states. He was acclaimed
everywhere. He arranged contracts for a considerable body of new
work; he noted all of his experiences, later to be published in *Those
United States* (1912); he returned to Europe in December much in

need of rest. He did not soon recover from the chill he had taken coming home; then, holidaying in the south of France, he suffered an attack thought to be gastroenteritis, but probably typhoid, which debilitated him further. He was to enjoy only short periods of improved health for the rest of his life.

Bennett now began to think of returning to live in England. He could afford a yacht and bought one called the *Velsa*. His travels in it he registered in *From the Log of the Velsa* (1914). He purchased a country estate called Comarques, at Thorpe-le-Soken, Essex, a Queen Anne house of great beauty. There he could live in the expansive style he admired and could entertain his many relatives and the multitude of his friends. He hired an excellent secretary, Miss Winnifred Nerney, who dedicated her life to his service from 1912 to his death. Her loyalty, efficiency, and valued judgments constantly supported Bennett's remarkable schedule of work. Nevertheless, these affluent years were less productive than usual. Then in 1914 the war broke out, and his mother, to whom he had written every day for twenty-five years, died.

In this period of crisis Bennett was spurred to complete the writing of *These Twain,* the third of the Clayhanger series, dealing with the experiences in marriage of the principal figures of the first two books. Informing the strength of feeling projected in the novel were the tensions always present in his own marriage, tensions which were increased in the war years to the breaking point. Bennett found himself drawn back to London, brought into close association with the newspaper magnate, Lord Beaverbrook, and inevitably forced into political activity.[20] He had begun, in August, 1914, to write a series of war articles for the *Daily News* which appeared almost every Thursday; he became a director of the *New Statesman* in April, 1915; he began a new serial called *The Lion's Share* for the *Strand;* and he began arrangements for a tour of the Western Front. In June the tour took place. His accounts for the *London Illustrated News* and *Saturday Evening Post,* later collected in a volume entitled *Over There* (1915), represent what he believed a responsible, patriotic, public figure should say. He did not speak of the horrors he saw; he did not wish to incite panic, or to cause despair. In November, 1916, he took a flat at his favorite club, The Royal Yacht Club, to be nearer the center of action.

Marguerite also took a flat of her own at Thackeray Mansions. They saw each other frequently in the city, still spent weekends

and Christmases together at Comarques, but it was becoming more
obvious that their marriage was breaking down, and that country
living was losing its appeal for Bennett. Aggravating the deteriorating relationship were all the extraordinary circumstances surrounding their informal adoption of Bennett's nephew Richard,
Frank's son, as their child.[21] From 1917 Marguerite tried to force
the teen-ager to love her and to relegate his parents to the level of
distant friends. Naturally, the boy's increasing resentment led in
1918 to his declaration of dislike for his aunt-mother and to her
hysterical abandonment of him. He was precipitately sent back to
his economically depressed parents. However, Bennett continued
to educate the boy and wrote constantly to him.[22]

   Within these years Bennett wrote *The Roll Call* (1918), an
unsuccessful sequel to the Clayhanger trilogy, and published *The
Pretty Lady* (1918) featuring a French cocotte. The latter caused a
furor in publishing and critical circles as a decadent and porno-
graphic book. Bennett enjoyed writing it. His discreet handling of
prostitution would not disturb readers today. His journalism in
these years attracted the admiration of W. M. Aitken, Lord
Beaverbrook, press lord, financier, and politician. Beaverbrook
particularly admired *The Pretty Lady* and drew from its presentation of French psychology the confidence to appoint Bennett
director of propaganda in France after Beaverbrook himself had
become Minister of Information in 1918. Bennett accepted the
post, found himself overwhelmed with work, but reveled in the
sense of actually doing something definite for the war effort, and
thoroughly delighted in the company of the beautiful, talented
socialites with whom Beaverbrook surrounded himself. When the
ministry ended following the Armistice, Bennett was offered a
knighthood, but refused it. He continued to visit Beaverbrook's
homes, to travel with him, even as far as Russia, and to share a
doughty friendship until his own death. Seven years after the war
Bennett was to create *Lord Raingo* from the experiences of those
years.

   The hectic postwar period found Bennett more involved than
ever in his theatrical obsession—writing *Judith* for Lilah Macarthy,
overseeing the production at the Aldwych Theatre of his dramatization of *Sacred and Profane Love,* assisting in the adaptation of *The
Beggar's Opera* which began a three-year run at the Lyric Theatre.
He also wrote in 1922 two lighter novels, *Mr. Prohack* and *Lillian*;

the first, a popular study of how a man copes with sudden wealth; the second, an unpopular fiction of a secretary who chooses free love and its consequences. Neither ranks with Bennett's best work.

He continued his extensive journalism and bought a larger yacht. He took a larger apartment in George Street, Hanover Square, where Marguerite could stay. He renamed the new yacht the *Marie Marguerite*, but his wife had always disliked sailing and resented Bennett's frequent trips without her. With no war work to engage her, she began again to throw herself into poetry readings, some in association with Edith Sitwell. At a recital given at Bedford College, the University of London, she met a French lecturer, Pierre Legros. Her friendship with Legros flourished. In March, 1921, she holidayed with him in Italy. By October the Bennetts were formally separated.

However the blame is to be apportioned for the disaster of this marriage, for by all accounts the experience was ravaging for both parties, it is clear that in ending it Bennett was exceedingly generous in his settlement with Marguerite and entirely gentlemanly toward her to the end of his life. He hoped now to be free. She, on the other hand, refused to divorce him, accepted all he would give and attempted to get more, published an embarrassing account of their marriage in a long series in the *Daily News*, constantly for years besieged his relatives to see her as the innocent, wronged wife, eleven years later intruded into the building where he lay dying in an upstairs apartment shared with the last love of his life, and marched in righteousness as his legal wife in the funeral procession to his grave in Burslem. It is hard not to view the difficult, unhappy Marguerite, in the constant extremes of her behavior, as an emotionally disturbed woman who had found the circumstances of marriage so incompatible with her romantic dreams that she could neither be an acceptable wife to Bennett nor grant him the freedom to live without her.

Bennett suffered another disruption in his life in 1922. J. B. Pinker, his invaluable, utterly trusted agent, died. They had never been very close, but Bennett's entire finances were managed by Pinker, his work had been tirelessly and cleverly promoted by him. Pinker's nephew, Eric, would continue to run the business, but Bennett did not feel secure with the younger man's management. Bennett was never again to be as economically stable as he had been; indeed, he was to become successively more worried about his financial state.

However, in that same year Bennett, in cultivating the friendships of attractive young artists like the pianist, Harriet Cohen, also met for the first time Dorothy Cheston Bennett,[23] a young actress who was to share the last eight years of his life and bear his only child. By the spring of the following year Bennett was ready to declare his love, make clear his marital situation, and offer her all he could. In this period he wrote *Riceyman Steps* (1923), a novel which restored flagging critical faith in him. He moved into a new home at 75 Cadogan Square, London. After completing the novel, and upon Dorothy's return from a theatrical engagement in Eastbourne, he decided to join her for a holiday in Paris. A month after their return to London, Dorothy made the decision to become his mistress. She came to know of the complicated nature of Bennett's household management and general arrangements, of his frequent illnesses and depressions. He came to know of her theatrical ambitions. However, they were both caught up in the whirl of social activities which always attracted Bennett, and in the theater which neither could resist. He helped her get suitable parts and fondly encouraged her ambitions. She received good reviews and dreamed of a great career.

The years of emotional and sexual satisfaction with Dorothy were attended by a rising tide of criticism from a new generation of writers. In many cases, Bennett provoked these attacks, thoroughly enjoying the effect of stirring up *"les jeunes,"* believing himself well able to parry their thrusts, and showing at all times an avuncular, but discriminating, interest in their development extending even to anonymous financial support. Some, like D. H. Lawrence,[24] who solicited money from Bennett, bitterly resented all he stood for; some, like Ezra Pound,[25] damned what they viewed as his materialism; some, like Virginia Woolf,[26] across class barriers, misunderstood his literature.

Early in 1925 Bennett began to create *Lord Raingo*. Before the completion of the novel he knew that 1926 would bring an astounding change into his life. Five years from his own death he was to become a father. His daughter, Virginia, was born on April 13, 1926, and from the first day delighted her father. Bennett and Dorothy hoped that now Marguerite would grant him a divorce. She, however, living well on his remarkably generous settlement, could not permit them so much happiness. Dorothy gained his name by deed poll only.

Bennett more than ever needed to earn money by his pen. He dashed off a sensational serial, *The Strange Vanguard* (1928), maintained his flow of journalism, had *Lord Raingo* (1926) published, began "Books and Persons," his well received series, for the *Evening Standard*, wrote another serialized novel, *Accident* (1928), and a collection of short stories entitled *The Women Who Stole Everything* (1927). He was happy in his productivity, contented in his new domestic life, and fascinated in his travels, the most recent trips being one with a group of male friends around the islands in the Mediterranean, followed by another trip to Berlin in Beaverbrook's party. He reread his thirty years of correspondence with his late estranged friend George Sturt, contemplating an edition of the letters. He supervised the Court Theatre's production of *Mr. Prohack*, the dramatization of his earlier novel in which Dorothy made her return to the stage after two years' absence for the baby. This production launched the successful career of Charles Laughton. Had the theater lease been longer, there appears no doubt but that the play would have had a long run; it could have given Dorothy that basis to reestablish her career; and it might then have provided Bennett considerable needed income. He also threw his remarkable energies into raising funds for the widow and children of Charles Masterman, an old associate of his. He planned a new play, *The Return Journey,* a new film, *Piccadilly,* a film script called *Punch and Judy* for the young director, Alfred Hitchcock, and a new serious novel, *Imperial Palace.* After more travels with Dorothy and Virginia in France and with Beaverbrook in Russia, he settled himself to concentrate upon his longest and, as it proved to be, his last completed novel.[27]

His final years were sadly worrying. He would not avoid the many responsibilities of being an important public figure, responsibilities which consumed much of his time. He refused to reduce the regimen of meeting his deadlines for journalism and correspondence. He could not refuse requests for various kinds of help from his family and many friends. He, who hated disruptions in his life, now had to move house. And he had to cope with Dorothy's and his theatrical disappointments, with his falling income, and with the rising costs of pre-depression years. Oppressed with anxieties, he made the bad decision to buy an apartment in

Chiltern Court, a new housing block immediately above an
underground railway. After moving there, he and Dorothy, tired
and dispirited, went to relax in France where twice Bennett drank
tap water knowing the risk he was taking. After three weeks, upon
his return to London, he began to show symptoms that were finally
diagnosed by a specialist as typhoid. All that could be done for him
was to make his decline as easy as possible. As a mark of the great
respect he commanded, the streets around Chiltern Court were
strewn with straw to deaden the traffic roar for the dying man.
Death came on March 27, 1931, two months after the onset of the
disease. After a service at the church of St. Clement Danes, his
ashes were interred in Burslem cemetery. In Margaret Drabble's
words: "his persuasively honest and amiable presence had departed,"[28] and all London mourned.

Bennett's Views of His Art

Throughout the thirty-seven years of his literary life Bennett
had studied the art of the novel. As a creative artist he had sought
for "beauty"; as a zealous craftsman, he had sought for "unity,"
"symmetry," "synthesis." From the study of Zola, the de Goncourts, Flaubert, and de Maupassant, he tried to produce verisimilitude in his novels. Impressed by Tolstoi, Turgenev, and
Dostoevski, he showed great compassion for his creatures. As an
appreciative reader of Henry Fielding, Jane Austen, and George
Meredith, he knew the value of humor in his prose. The resolution
into a coherent theory of the novel of the differences inherent in
these aims never exercised Bennett's mind. In 1902 he said:
"Although the habit of theorising about their art is not one to be
encouraged among artists—few of those who create with distinction can invent even reasonable theories to explain the instinctive
operation of their genius—it is nevertheless to be regretted that
more literary artists, especially those of the higher sort, do not talk
at large about their work, setting out the history of imaginative
inceptions and conclusions without attempting to lay down rules
or make generalizations."[29] As late as 1920, in the Introduction to
Edward Wadsworth's *The Black Country*, he continued to follow his
precept against legislating. "I am not such a simpleton as to attempt
a definition of art," he said. "Assuredly I am not such a simpleton
as to attempt a definition of beauty." But then he added: "I don't

mind asserting that beauty is everywhere, and that there is naught in which beauty is not."[30] Although he cannot be numbered among the important theorists of the novel, he made statements throughout his career that, when gathered together, show him to be generally consistent in aim.

His early fascination with technique places him among those English writers who in the 1890s were trying to create a "New Form" for the novel, and looked to France for direction. There, experimentation in painting and music provided as much stimulus as innovations in literature; in fact, the work of the Impressionist and Postimpressionist painters and musicians soon influenced young English writers away from simpler forms of realism. Ford Madox Ford and Joseph Conrad are more readily seen as heralding Impressionism in English fiction. Ford, who accepted the title of Impressionist, years later recalled the excitement of the time: "There was writing before Flaubert; but Flaubert and his coterie opened, as it were, a window through which one saw the literary scene from an entirely new angle. Perhaps more than anything else it was a matter of giving visibility to your pages; perhaps better than elsewhere, Conrad with his 'It is above all to make you see!' expressed the aims of the New World."[31]

Bennett, from the year of his arrival in London, was abreast of the trend, as Ford recognized. He reveled in gallery exhibitions of the Impressionist and Postimpressionist schools. He was aware of the reaction to the verisimilitude that in painting had led to the mechanical sterility of the academicians, and in fiction had led to the fact-mongering of the Naturalists. He soon turned from what he thought to be merely the surface interest of painters like Sisley, Manet, Monet, and looked in admiration at Cezanne[32] who tried to catch on canvas essential forms underlying surface reality, whose chosen images became much more than mirror reflections. Bennett believed that: "Superficial facts are of small importance . . . , they might, for the sake of more clearly disclosing the beauty, suffer a certain *distortion* . . ." (Journal, 1:84 January 3, 1899). He sought inspiration in performances of Saint-Saens, Debussy, Borodin, and Ravel—the latter was to become a personal friend. Far from being a dated traditionalist, Bennett was knowledgeable of the new modes, although he chose to draw the boundaries for himself more narrow than would please Virginia Woolf. In a Journal 1 entry (September 29, 1896), he more confidently identified the direction he would take. He said: "I have unwisely been reading books by George Meredith and Mrs. Humphrey Ward, and at first my work will certainly reflect their methods—methods which—the one splendidly fantastic, the other realistic by dint of laborious and carefully ordered detail are both at variance with my natural instincts towards a *synthetic impressionism.* I ought during the past month to have read nothing but de Goncourt."

Two years later, in another Journal 1 entry (January 11, 1898), Bennett expressed his recognition of French influence: "As regards fiction, it seems to me that only within the last few years have we absorbed from France that passion for the artistic shapely presentation of truth, and that feeling for words as words, which animated Flaubert, the de Goncourts, and de Maupassant, and which is so exactly described and defined in de Maupassant's introduction to the collected works of Flaubert. . . . An artist must be interested primarily in presentment, not in the thing presented. He must have a passion for technique, a deep love for form."

In the following year (*Journal 1* January 3, 1899), he recorded a modification of his view: "The day of my enthusiasm for 'realism,' for 'naturalism,' has passed. I can perceive that a modern work of fiction dealing with modern life may ignore realism and yet be great. To find beauty, which is always hidden; that is the aim. . . . My desire is to depict the deeper beauty while abiding by the envelope of facts."

In studying varieties of English realism Bennett perceived possibilities that further freed him to follow his own bent. In an *Academy* article on George Gissing written late in the same year he said:

The artists who have courage fully to exploit their own temperaments are always sufficiently infrequent to be peculiarly noticeable and welcome. Still more rare are they who, leaving it to others to sing and emphasize the ideal and obvious beauties which all can in some measure see, will exclusively exercise the artists' prerogative as an explorer of hidden and recondite beauty in unsuspected places . . . The spirit of the sublime dwells not only in the high and remote, it shines unperceived amid all the usual meannesses of our daily existence.[33]

Much later, in *Literary Taste,* he said: "The spirit of literature is unifying; it joins the candle and the star, and by the magic of an image shows that the beauty of the greater is in the less. And, not content with the disclosure of beauty and the bringing together of all things whatever within its focus, it enforces a moral wisdom by the tracing everywhere of cause and effect."[34] And later again in *The Author's Craft* he said: "An ugly deed—such as a deed of cruelty—takes on artistic beauty when its origin and hence its fitness in the general scheme begins to be comprehended."[35] Bennett's idea of beauty starts with the recognition of a pattern in events which must be revealed by the artist in that which is organized through careful selection; that which is a synthesis of facts achieved through an understanding of the basis of selection. Significant also in terms of his practice is the comparison he draws, in the passage just quoted, to explain the function of literature. Through organized imagery, the small, the insignificant, the lowly, the ordinary, can be shown to hold beauties that exist in the large, the significant, the illustrious, the extraordinary.

So much did this viewpoint dominate his thinking that he could be stirred to the depths of his being upon watching a ship pass through locks in a canal (*Journal* 1:45-50); yet he would look upon an alpine scene as "an immense quantity of the earth's surface . . . wasted by nature" serving "no purpose save to impress the unaccustomed eye."[36] That which had come under the dominion of man, that which was controlled for a purpose, stimulated his artistic endeavors and directed his study of his fellow human beings to those areas where their activities had created an environment wholly disparate from the haunts of nature—the Potteries, the narrow side streets of London, the great department stores and hotels of the city center. In an early letter to H. G. Wells he said: "It seems to me that there are immense possibilities in the very romance of manufacture—not wonders of machinery and that sort of stuff—but in the tremendous altercation with nature that is continually going on."[37]

Grappling with daily reality in an effort to find hidden beauty led Bennett to contemplate the nature of truth in fiction. In *Literary Taste*[38] he said that: "to disturb the spirit is one of the greatest aims of art"; that "honesty, in literature as in life, is the quality that counts first and counts last"; and explains, "of course, I use the word 'true' in a wide and essential significance. I do not necessarily mean true to literal fact; I mean true to the plane of experience in which the book moves." These statements emphasize Bennett's

belief that the successful search for beauty is directly related to the
artist's ability to observe clearly and accurately, to correlate
significantly, so that from the artist's compassionate treatment of
his material is created the impressive, that is, the disturbing and
truthful, work of art.

I hesitate to agree when James Hepburn states that indeed
beauty and truth are synonymous to Bennett and that this leads
Bennett into ambiguities in distinguishing between two kinds of
beauty—a beauty in technical arrangement and "beauty which the
artists' shaping mind has discerned in reality."[39] He goes on to say
that Bennett has contrived his "subjective-objective paradox that
an intensity of vision, a shaping vision, is required of the artist, and
yet that beauty inheres in reality." There can be no doubt that
some of Bennett's statements require a clarification that he did not
choose to give. Certainly the terms are closely related as understood by Bennett. He could not discover beauty without realizing
truth. Nevertheless, the combined weight of his statements makes
it reasonably apparent that Bennett believed that beauty inheres in
the circumstances of existence for the novelist to observe and
comprehend, and a different beauty resides in the novelist's
shaping vision; but he believed that truth appears in the moral
wisdom gained by the reader who has fully assimilated the writer's
creation. To say that beauty inhering in reality, and the beauty
created by the artist's shaping vision of reality, and the truth
revealed through the artist's creative organization are all one, is to
confuse cause, effect, and meaning. Bennett was not so confused.
In fact, he felt that Keats's dictum that beauty is truth, and truth is
beauty, was the kind of "airy"[40] linking that left the profound
definitions of these words unexpressed. But consistent with his
dislike of legislating, Bennett leaves the terms undefined.

Of primary importance in the search for "beauty" in such
unprepossessing districts as he chose is careful observation, an
important aim of both the realists and Impressionists. Bennett
claimed: "The great artist may force you to laugh or to wipe away a
tear, but he accomplishes these minor feats by the way. What he
mainly does is to *see* for you."[41] He entitled Part 1 of *The Author's
Craft*, "Seeing Life." In it he makes clear that observation is much
more than looking and making an annotated list of trivial facts. He
exhorted the writer "to realise that all physical phenomena are
inter-related, that there is nothing which does not bear on

everything else"[42] therefore, "good observation consists not in multiplicity of detail, but in coordination of detail according to a true perspective of relative importance, so that a finally just general impression may be reached in the shortest possible time".[43] He concluded that every street is a mirror, an illustration, an exposition, an explanation, of the human beings who live in it".[44] The essential unity in human affairs, which is there to be observed and which, when recognized by the sensitive writer, enables him to represent cause and effect in events, is, for Bennett, the prime source of beauty in fiction. Unity understood in these terms supported his belief that man has choice, but the area of choice is circumscribed by the acts of one's forebears and fellows and by fluctuations in mores. Therefore, his desire to depict developments over more than one generation emphasizes his wish to reveal the causes and effects of events determined by choices made in these circumstances, in order to increase the reader's compassion and give him a greater awareness of his scope in living intelligently.

But the nature of seeing, of gaining a true perspective, of recognizing unity, of representing truth through beauty, is not a mechanical objectivism, nor a cold realism. In January, 1897, Bennett said: "Every scene, even the commonest, is wonderful, if only one can detach oneself, casting off all memory of use and custom, and behold it (as it were) for the first time; in its right, authentic colours; without making comparisons. The novelist should cherish and burnish this faculty of seeing crudely, simply, artlessly, ignorantly; of seeing like a baby or a lunatic, who lives each moment by itself and tarnishes the present by no remembrance of the past (*Journal*, 1:28). Three years later he wrote in the *Academy* article on J. M. Barrie: "If, in presenting a scene, he [the artist] does not disclose aspects of it which you would not have observed for yourself, then he falls short of success. In a physical and psychical sense his power is visual, the power of an eye seeing things always afresh, virginally, as though on the very morn of creation itself."[45]

Bennett in the *Journal* statement expressed a major principle of the Impressionists almost a year before Conrad published his famous Preface to *The Nigger of the Narcissus*. Both the first and second quotations impress upon the reader Bennett's desire to attempt a communication of a view of life that would penetrate the surfaces without dispensing with them. Taken together, these statements are not to be understood as merely isolating each scene observed from what had existed before and from what might follow after, as one modern critic has assumed.[46] The first, modified by the second, shows that Bennett wanted to *see* the individual phenomenon for what it really is in order to give it its place in the pattern of life. The abstracting view is to be valued for the clarity it gives to the process of preparing a "synthetic map" and, in the end, to the clarity of the "map" itself. "The makers of literature," Bennett said in 1909, "are those who have seen and felt the miraculous interestingness of the universe. . . . Not isolated and unconnected parts of life, but all of life, brought together and correlated in a synthetic map."[47] The aim is awareness and understanding.

In "seeing" and "synthesizing" the attitude of the author was of utmost importance to Bennett. Throughout his published writing he reiterated his recognition that the creative artist observes idiosyncratically—that any attempt to preserve a clinical impersonality would result in a mechanical presentation false to nature in its particularity. In another *Academy* article written in 1901 he said: "It is a characteristic of the literary artist with a genuine vocation that his large desire is, not to express in words any particular thing, but to express *himself*, the sum of his sensations."[48] In *Literary Taste* he claimed: "The book is nothing but the man trying to talk to you, trying to impart to you some of his feelings,"[49] and, in *The Author's Craft* he said: "Just as individuals are singled out from systems, in the earlier process of observation, so in the later processes individuals will be formed into new groups, which formation will depend upon the personal bent of the observer."[50] However, the "personal bent of the observer" was to include a characteristic important to Bennett and typical of him as man and author. In one of his earlier *Journal* entries (October 15, 1896) he defined as "Essential characteristics of the really great novelist: a Christ-like, all-embracing compassion"; in 1909 (*Literary Taste*, p. 121) he said the reader must be helped "to understand all and forgive all"; and echoed his credo in *The Author's Craft* (1914, p. 63) where he called for a "universal sympathy."

Knowledge of the truth, "moral wisdom," was not to be gained or communicated through any form of parsonical approach, however. Bennett disliked preachment or moralizing in novels and criticized George Eliot and others for this fault. Bennett was gradually to recognize the value to him of the all-embracing approach to comedy. He was to "see," as it were, through the eyes of George Meredith's Comic Spirit. It is mainly in his novels themselves that the proof of the validity of this statement can be found. Although for years underestimating his flair for comedy, partly because of the ease with which comic methods came to him, partly because he relegated his natural facility for writing broad farce, blatant satire, and slapstick comedy to earning money, Bennett, nevertheless, early recognized the breadth of comedy. In an *Academy* article, he said: "The distinction between comedy and farce is that, while comedy must be faithful to nature and probability, farce may use any means towards the end of hilarity. A comedy should show the effect of character on character, of character on event, and of event on character. It may be either serious (on this side of tragedy) or humorous, or both."[51] In *The Author's Craft,* that work of his mid-years, he never specifically assigned the importance to comedy that his practice proves. However, as he had gradually come to attach "less and less importance to good technique in fiction" because he had gradually come to place primary importance on an attribute of the writer— "fineness of mind"—he said: "[The writer's] mind must be sympathetic, quickly responsive, courageous, honest, humorous, tender, just, merciful. He must be able to conceive the ideal without losing sight of the fact that it is a human world we live in."[52] These words give expression to what was his comic credo. With this approach Bennett could look closely and clearly at the Black Country and the streets of London and see and project a profound view of the comedy of life.

Chapter Two
Advance From Melodrama

Before Bennett published *The Old Wives' Tale*, his first generally acclaimed masterpiece, he wrote sixteen other novels. The first five of these form a significant group for analysis. They are *A Man from the North* (1898),[1] his first substantial effort; *The Ghost* (1907),[2] a melodramatic tale; *The Gates of Wrath* (1903),[3] a caricature of the melodramatic type; *The Grand Babylon Hotel* (1902),[4] an exuberant detective story; and *Anna of the Five Towns* (1902),[5] his first critical success. The order is not based upon the chronology of publication, but is based upon the major creative periods as determined from Bennett's journals and letters. Bennett distinguished between his various novels, calling some "serious," as *A Man* and *Anna*; calling others "melodramas," as *The Gates of Wrath*; calling still others "fantasias," as *The Ghost* and *The Grand Babylon Hotel*; and calling one book a "frolic," *A Great Man* (1904). Often, these terms appear as subtitles indicating Bennett's general aim in each. If the order of publication of all Bennett's novels is examined, the serious and non-serious are seen to be usually alternated. Bennett stressed the importance of this arrangement in a directive to his agent, J. B. Pinker.[6] He believed that his serious novels showed his artistry, and that his light work, though not "scamped," could never rank with his best. Nevertheless, he believed that writing sensational serials gave an aspiring author opportunities to perfect much of the author's craft.[7] He found that his lighter work was a necessary relief from, and stimulation to, the creative effort demanded by his serious work.

Publishing in alternations each year is generally adhered to insofar as Bennett successfully continued his amazing writing schedule and the vagaries of the publishing businesses allowed. However, after Bennett wrote his first serious novel, he wrote three light works before he turned again to his more important studies. He expressed two reasons for this difference in pattern: "Till the end of 1899 I propose to give myself absolutely to writing the sort of fiction that sells itself. My serious novel 'Anna

Tellwright' with which I have made some progress is put aside
indefinitely—or rather until I have made seen what I can do."[8]
What he did was to attempt a melodrama, then returned to the
kind of caricature that had first won him a prize and given him
the confidence to start an author's career, and then gave himself
the free range of writing a humorous detective story. In these
varying modes Bennett started to sharpen, among other tools, the
tool of an effective comic technique. *Anna*, therefore, is a
considerable advance over Bennett's achievement in *A Man*. The
advance is toward a greater awareness of his deepest feelings about
humanity shown through a greater subtlety in ironic presentation
and an increase in the use of gentle humor, with a further
clarification of the theme of illusion versus reality that Bennett
considered throughout his life.

A Man From the North

The first chapter of *A Man*[9] presents the two significant features
in the narrative: the character of the central figure and the attitude
of the onmiscient narrator. The chapter is a brief philosophical
foreword to the story of Richard Larch in which his inexperienced
dreaming nature is made clear through an unobtrusive ironic point
of view. The course of the narrative is implied and all is accomplished with the greatest brevity in an apparently uncontrived
simple statement.

The approach is in keeping with Bennett's attitude toward his
craft at the time. In the 1890s he valued a presentation of the gray
life of ordinary individuals in a form that did not glamorize,
whitewash, or blacken. However, he had an instinctive desire to be
compassionate and a belief that the truthful artist must take the
freedom to shape events in order to create intelligible form for the
truths he sees and understands. Considerable effort to give a
pattern to Richard's development distinguishes Bennett's treatment.

The narrative features four figures: Richard; Mr. Aked, a
solicitor's clerk in London; Aked's niece, Adeline, who keeps
house for him; and Laura Roberts, a cashier in a restaurant Aked
frequents. Appearances are made by Jenkins, a junior clerk in
Aked's office, and a nurse who attended Aked's last illness. A few

other characters make briefer appearances or are merely referred
to at appropriate places in the development of the plot.

An examination of events reveals an emphasis upon three major
areas of Richard's life in London—his literary efforts, his office
work, and his relations with women. In the first six chapters
Richard's literary aspirations are developed from vague dreams to
more definite aims which are given some particularity through an
acquaintance with Aked. The seventh chapter presents his promotion at work and his first meeting with Laura. In chapter 27
Richard's next major promotion comes in the same chapter as his
first major move toward her. The intervening chapters present his
literary efforts and his attempts to discover what Adeline could
mean to him. Almost evenly spaced in the development of these
chapters are two glimpses of Laura and two statements of Richard's
steady progress at work. Not yet able or willing to see the realities
of his situation, he makes his most ambitious and, he believes, his
most desperate effort to become an author. In the remaining
chapters he recognizes Laura's appeal to him, courts her, and
proposes. The final chapter presents his reflections upon his
decision. He is not joyous because he still clings to the belief that
nature had denied him strength of purpose and that his situation
might and should have been different.

The pattern of the novel emphasizes the growth to one level of
maturity of a man who will be nothing more than the ordinary
householder, the plodding husband and father who trails tatters of
dreams that dignify him for having had them. Basically he simply
lacked the talent to follow his dreams. His talents direct him
elsewhere. The course of the novel presents that aspect of reaching
for the moon that is part of many temperaments. A comparison of
the facts of the narrative with Bennett's biography of the period
reveals parallels and opposites that add meaning to his presentation. His creation of Richard Larch is an exaggeration of much that
he feared might develop in his own situation.

Upon first reading, comedy may not appear to be an important
element. Yet comic techniques are used at significant points
throughout the narrative. The tale is a comedy in the broadest and
simplest sentimental tradition in that it ends with a proposed
marriage. But there are ambiguities in the ending which make it
impossible to categorize the nature of the narrative even in that

superficial way. Much more significant is the fact that throughout the novel Richard is treated with humor.

When walking in central London within hours of his arrival, he is feeling "acutely happy" at the naive thought that "London accepted him"(7). Just as his elation makes him conscious of being "filled with great purposes"(8), he had mud flung in his face from a passing cab. Richard's reaction is to wipe it off "caressingly, with a smile"(7). The reader must smile too at the good spirits of the inexperienced youth. At the same time the reader is aware that the presumption of Richard's thought that London accepts him and the vague optimism of his "great purpose" are answered by his getting London mud in the eye.

Richard's inexperience and his need to feel adequate to his dreams of his future are presented in little incidents remarkable for their truth to life and for the humorous understanding they give the reader. In his first stroll around central London Richard notices a trinket shop. Needing to feel that he belongs, he enters, gruffly requests to see, and purchases, a watch. Bennett concludes, "And he walked out, putting his purchase in his pocket. A perfectly reliable gold watch, which he had worn for years, already lay there" (9). The little shock of surprise followed by an amused sympathy is neatly stimulated. The effect is similar to endings Maupassant gave many of his short stories and reminds one that Bennett was avidly reading French masters. The development of Richard's character is attended throughout by similar effects. Not all instances are softened by sympathy. The direct irony of the statement, "Richard sat down to be an author" (34), forces the reader to stand apart from the dreaming youth and judge him presumptuous. The reader need never take Richard's ambitions as seriously as Richard wishes to do.

But comedy in the smaller details used as illustrations above serves to emphasize only Bennett's more obvious methods of revealing Richard's character and immaturity. In less obvious ways comedy appears in the patterning of events around Bennett's theme. The three major aspects of the North Country youth's life in London have already been mentioned: his literary ambitions, his office work, his acquaintanceship with women. The novel has frequently been interpreted as the study of a young provincial with literary ambitions who is crushed into a bourgeois nonentity by circumstances and a lack of strength of will. One is led to think that of the three aspects listed, the first is of primary importance, and the loss of ambition constitutes a pathetic, if not a tragic, conclusion to the novel. In fact, the weight of chapters dealing with these aspects proves that it is the development of the third—Richard's association with women—that provides the bulk of the book, and the result is not tragic, or even necessarily pathetic.

Richard was reared by his sister in Bursley, lived in London at the boardinghouse of a probable widow and her daughter, is obsessed by the sights and sounds of women wherever he chances to meet them, has only two male friends in London, and finally is drawn into relatively close association with three contrasting female types: Adeline, the pretty, practical, passive one; a nurse, the brisk, efficient, accomplished one; and Laura, the simple, dependent, passionate one. The course of events provides the spectacle of a young man, with notions of grandeur, ignoring his instincts to the point where he tries hard to make Adeline fit an image he has created of her, and tries even harder to fall in love with this image. The events show his irritation with the second girl who actually has many of the attributes and talents he wished to find in Adeline. Finally, the events reveal how he ignores all the signs of his honest attraction to Laura because of his aspirations until circumstances appear to force his capitulation.

One is provoked to smile at much in the young man's passage from country-hopeful to middle-class city husband and prospective father. There is no emphasis upon outstanding events or outstanding characters. But the reader watches the tentative character of Richard Larch lose a little of its tentativeness under the press of circumstances and his psychological needs in daily living. Bennett's insight is noteworthy, his handling of his material generally deft. At the peak of his career he said, "For twelve years I have consistently stuck up for this book, as having a quality which none of my other books has, & of course now that some interest is being shown in it, I am more in love with it than ever."[10] The quality that marks the novel is his concentration upon character development revealed through the gradual massing of insignificant details which with careful phrasing and placing gain significance.

George Lafourcade has shrewdly assessed Bennett's modernity in developing "contradiction" or "emotional discontinuity" and "regression"[11] in his characters. But Lafourcade discusses this tendency only in later novels. It is possible to see the beginnings of this aspect in Richard Larch whose innate sensuality wars against his artistic aspirations. Much of Richard's unrecognized needs and desires are as clearly presented as those he is more conscious of, or talks about. There is not much complication because Richard is still a considerably raw, practically untried youth as the novel ends. The substantive "man" in the title is ironic.

Bennett's conclusions about character-drawing in fiction are given in a lengthy *Journal* entry[12] the day after he had a long chat with T. S. Eliot. The two men had agreed that a character had to be conventionalized to form part of the pattern, although it brought the criticism that in such conventionalization there was no character-drawing at all. The need was to create an impression of the truth. They felt that the newest "despisers of form . . . produce no impression at all." Although these opinions were written in 1924, the reader of *A Man* can see the germ of them in its characterization.

Two less important aspects require brief comment—set descriptions and symbolism. A description opening the sixth chapter captures city sounds in the summer heat. Bennett's method goes further than make clear the particular condition of his hero on the particular evening in question. The direct contrast between the languor that the rhythm of the passage catches and the abruptness of the opening of the following paragraph has the double effect of indicating Richard's immediate need to draw his thoughts back from mountains or sea and start work. And it draws attention to the irony of his attempt. It is possible to conclude that Bennett gave set descriptions more than local value; that, in fact, they also serve to explicate, with varying emphases, one of his major themes, illusion versus reality. Through the frequent use of direct contrast between the set scene and the hero's particular mental and emotional situation the descriptions serve the comic mode through which the meanings of Richard's story are made clear.

Symbolism, the final point to be mentioned, does not rank with those points presented so far. Only one fairly obvious symbol will be referred to. The linking of important events, decisions, and the like, to the image of a bridge that has not been crossed by the lone figure near it or on it recurs in *A Man* and in many of Bennett's

novels, taking on, in later works like *Clayhanger*, symbolic significance. A full discussion of the point cannot be attempted here. To
conclude, all the cited elements indicate that *A Man From the North*
is a distinguished first novel.

Three Sensational Serials: *The Ghost, The Gates of Wrath,* and *The Grand Babylon Hotel*

Bennett's second novel, *The Ghost,*[13] depicts the adventure of
Carl Foster, a young Scottish medical graduate, who, upon coming
to London, meets his cousin Sullivan Smith and becomes em-
broiled in the lives of the musical comedy stars Rosa and Alresca.
Alresca mysteriously dies, Rosa has her rival make an attempt on
her life, and Carl discovers that any man attracted to Rosa is
haunted by her dead lover, Lord Clarenceaux. After many trials
Rosa supplicates to the ghost for Carl and succeeds. Obviously
there are few parallels in this work that suggest the achievement of
A Man.

Bennett subtitled the novel "A Fantasia on Modern Themes"
and intended to follow the pattern of sensational serial writing that
he later laid down in *How to Become an Author* (1903). He would
start the story straight off with no preliminaries; he would have
exotic characters; there would be no attempt to render subtleties
of character; there would be theatrical dialogue, swift changes of
scene, and scenes exotically contrasted. Also, the artificial divisions of serial publication must be met—roughly, every two
chapters making an installment must create a minor crisis at the
end to keep readers in suspense for the next issue. There is more
informal dialogue in this novel than in *A Man.* "Give the public
what they want, and save half your income—that's the ticket,"
Sullivan Smith says (10), in a reduced echo of Wilkie Collins's
famous dictum. It is Bennett's aim also in writing *The Ghost.*
However, Bennett shows his desire to make something different
of the melodrama in that he chose to set almost the first hundred
pages of the book in the center of London's theatrical world, with
many people, bright lights, jostling crowds, brilliant colors, the
very opposite to the dark moors, solitary houses, and strange
individuals that formed the stock in trade of writers of ghostly
tales.

The device of delineating conversations and events, with the occasional appearance of humor, within which a strange incident is set, gradually builds up a credibility for the reality of the ghostly appearances. This method is augmented by the youthful hero's continual effort to rationalize his experiences as the result of thought transference, or of hypnotic suggestion. From the first appearance of the ghost to Carl on a London street it is treated as a real man and not a figment of the hero's imagination. These devices have a cumulative effect which give the extremely melodramatic plot a unique presentation. However, no attempt is made to realize a consistent use of all the comic devices for an artistic end. It may be supposed that, among other flaws, Bennett's failure to integrate comic modes with the tale of the supernatural led him to say of the novel much later in his career that it represented a good idea insufficiently developed.

While *The Ghost* was appearing serially, Bennett wrote his third novel, another melodramatic tale called *The Gates of Wrath*.[14] This book is completely ignored by the latest criticism of Bennett, or is dismissed as a novel having every conceivable flaw. The point missed by its modern critics, although some of its earliest reviewers recognized the presence of entertaining humor, is that Bennett is diverting himself with a parody of the sensational serial melodrama, and all stops are pulled. Bennett already had some experience in caricature. It is not surprising that, after writing one melodrama with humorous inclusions, he pokes fun at the genre in his next publication.

The Gates of Wrath presents the machinations of Dr. Colpus and Mrs. Cavalossi to secure Arthur Forrest's wealth by having him marry Mrs. Cavalossi's daughter. A marriage between the hero and heroine, usually the culmination of the popular serial, occurs at the beginning of Bennett's tale. This is the only part of the villains' plot that succeeds. After Arthur has married Sylviane, the villains learn that he will not claim his wealth. It is to go to his half brother. The villains realize they will have to arrange the deaths of two men. They bungle all arrangements. The plot from this point is contrived to have the hero and heroine win over the villains. Each character is made to epitomize a stock melodramatic type. The descriptions are cliché-ridden parodies of melodramatic techniques. Two other characters, Arthur Peterson, the half-mad half brother of the hero, and Simms, henchman of Dr. Colpus, make up the cast.

The culmination of the story has all the trappings of the gothic tale, but the trappings are all illusory. Peterson takes his guests one moonlit night to the construction site of his new mansion. The unfinished building appears like "some immense and age-worn ruin" (184) wrapped in uncanny silence. They climb the scaffolding as if mounting through the turns of stairs in an old tower. As Peterson begins to lead them over to the other side of the construction, he disappears without a sound. Unable to suppress fears of the supernatural, Sylviane and Arthur grope their way to the ground, but find Peterson extricating himself from a sandpile. This anticlimax emphasizes Bennett's satirical aim. The three characters return to the country house where Sylviane implicates Peter's valet, Simms, as an accomplice of the villains. Arthur approaches Simms and gains a full confession by pulling a gun out of a paper bag. Obviously, the narrative was treated as a caricature in which Bennett could make fun of every aspect of the typical tale of villains. He can be credited with the judgment that his ability to write satirically was wasted upon attacking narratives typical of the "penny-dreadfuls."

The Grand Babylon Hotel,[15] the third of the serials, presents Racksole, an American multimillionaire and Nella, his daughter, involved in murder, kidnapping, attempted suicide, rivalries between two German principalities, and all because the millionaire bought Felix Babylon's hotel in London so that his willful daughter might have the dinner she wishes to have on her first night there. The absurdly improbable is once again the principal cause of laughter in the novel. *The Grand Babylon Hotel* presents melodrama as a boundless source of lighthearted laughter, and simultaneously the vehicle of an ingenious detective story. Bennett misses no trick to wring every ounce of humor out of all the situations he can devise to unfold the tale.

Chapter 2 introduces most of the threads of the mystery to be developed and finally solved. Out of Racksole's meeting with Felix Babylon, the hotel changes hands, the new owner is warned of the mysteries shrouded in all hotels, Jules is properly made to serve the steak and bass, Nella learns of the astounding transaction necessary to satisfy her whim, she introduces her father to

Reginald Dimmock, equerry to Prince Aribert of Posen who is soon to arrive at the hotel. The chapter concludes as Jules covertly winks at Dimmock, a wink not lost upon either Racksole or his alert daughter.

The first installment was calculated to amuse and intrigue the popular taste. The attractive fairy-tale quality of the narrative is increased by the amusing unorthodoxy of the father-daughter relationship of the two major figures. Within the chapter, when Racksole seeks out Felix Babylon to talk of the internal workings of the hotel, Bennett begins to reveal the fascination that the organization of the world within a hotel had for him, a fascination which lasted throughout his life. He gradually builds up the belief that a hotel is a very complex world indeed and, contrary to ordinary opinion, an appropriate place for the occurrence of the most fearful deeds.

From chapter 3 onward, the strange incidents multiply. Scenes of hidden stairwells, shadowy wine cellars, gambling casinos, provide appropriate locales for the multiple treacheries involved. Finally, with Jules identified as the master criminal, Racksole arranges for the Thames to be searched by an old friend of his at the Customs House. An exciting river chase ends in Jules's capture, but he is killed in an escape attempt. Prince Eugen's life is saved when he hears that Racksole will make him a needed loan, and his brother, Prince Aribert, is free to marry a commoner with Eugen safely married on the throne of Posen. He asks Racksole for Nella's hand, and Felix Babylon asks Racksole for his hotel again. All is satisfactorily settled, and all has transpired during the period of the millionaire's holiday. The story is worked out to include almost every conceivable situation that might titillate the reading public. Many of its early reviewers recognized the ingenuity of the clustering incidents and thoroughly enjoyed the good fun of the humorous presentation of them.

A reflection upon the development of Bennett's first four novels enables one to see that, by the time he came to write *Anna*, he had considerably advanced his technical ability in devising plot, in dramatic presentation, in distinguishing character, and in the use of comic devices. From the too objective irony of his approach to Richard Larch's less serious dilemma, and from the free and often careless use of comic devices to link the extraordinary with the

ordinary for superficial ends in the melodramas, he could now
subdue comedy to aid him in relating sympathetically, and movingly, the realities of a common life.

Anna of the Five Towns

Anna of the Five Towns presents an exploration of the problem of
the subtly drawn character of the eldest daughter of Ephraim
Tellwright, wealthy miser of Bursley, one of the "five towns" of the
Potteries. So subtly is her character depicted that H. G. Wells
criticized it, saying: "On the whole I should describe my impression as being that of a photograph a little under-developed." To
which Bennett confidently retorted: "As to the under-developed
photograph, this is largely a matter of taste. But I trust you
understand that the degree of development to which I have
brought the photograph, is what I think the proper degree. It is
Turgenev's degree, and Flaubert's. It is *not* Balzac's." Wells is
moved to say after further consideration that "*Anna* I find ripens in
the mind."[16] The art with which Bennett makes the story immediately appealing and filled with stores that "ripen in the mind"
marks his first significant step toward the mastery of his craft for
his particular purpose.

The story presents the period of Anna Tellwright's courtship
and betrothal to Henry Mynors, a man deemed by her society
eminently worthy to marry the heiress. Out of the grayness of her
monotonous existence as a virtual slave to her father and the
grayness of the marriage into which she goes, the few months
depicted in the novel stand apart as bright and filled with compelling emotion. The period includes her coming of age, her receipt
of a large inheritance, her first trip away from home, the suicide of
the Sunday School superintendent, who was also her tenant, her
betrothal to Henry Mynors, her one great act of defiance to her
father in aid of Willie Price, her recognition of their mutual love,
Willie's departure, her resignation to a marriage of duty, and,
unknown to her, Willie's death.

Around these events the multiple activities of the industrial
town are woven in a way that emphasizes the inseparableness of
the individual life from that of the masses, and the power of
heredity and environment to shape the unique individual to
conform to the pattern. The fact that the individual preserves the

power to be true to herself in spite of all influences that could smother the impulse is made the crisis of the story. The tragic propensities of ordinary existence are indicated by the fact that Anna's impulse to be true to herself finds only a momentary expression, one single act, before she sinks back into the blanketing folds of habit.

Quite new in this novel is Bennett's selection of a brief series of events that are powerfully interconnected and that completely illuminate the life of the heroine and the society of which she is helplessly a part. There is no outside fate manipulating affairs into tragedy; there is no serious dependence upon chance to lead to a climax. Instead, Bennett manages through closely woven detail to show how the course of events in a particular society is naturally caused and has its necessary and consistent conclusion. In *A Man* there is a lack of events made significant. And although the characters are few, the reader knows them far less than he learns to know Anna and her circle. But the greatest difference between the two novels is that in *A Man* neither the hero nor any of his experiences has an essential connection with London. Whereas, in *Anna*, the setting of the Potteries is crucial to an understanding of the heroine and of the meaning of her story.

This is not to brand the novel "regional" with the usual limitation implied. Rather, it is to emphasize that once Bennett had arrived at the point of development where he had the technical ability to say something important about living, he had also the wisdom to realize that he would find the means of saying it through a contemplation of the people in the place where his own roots were deepest. This explains why he chose as an inscription for the novel the Wordsworthian lines: "Therefore, although it be a history / Homely and rude, I will relate the same / For the delight of a few natural hearts." Just as in *Michael* Wordsworth wished to tap the "essential passions," to trace the "primary laws of our nature," and chose his rural shepherd through whose life he could make these things clear to his readers, so Bennett chose Anna. But there is an irony involved, for Wordsworth believed that humble and rustic life provided a level on which the essential passions functioned beneficiently without restraint, while Bennett chose to depict the coils of repression which burden small-town life.

To tell this tale of frustration and stoical endurance, Bennett created a plot that is a considerable advance over that of *A Man*.

Richard's dilemma disappears when he is forced to recognize where his strengths really lie. Much more compelling is the plot that delineates Anna's more significant dilemma between her moral principles and the needs and desires of her character and temperament. Richard creates his own problem arbitrarily; Anna's problem cannot be disassociated from her milieu. In developing her problem Bennett is exploring one closely related to his own psychology, and one which, in varying forms, has always beset man in society.

In fourteen chapters the events are concentrated; each one following the other in an inevitable pattern through which the descriptive imagery is used sparingly but with significant point. Thus, it is through the candid eyes of a child that Henry Mynors and Willie Price, unwitting rivals for Anna's love, first appear to the reader. One remembers Bennett's exhortation, in another context, to look upon life with the untrammeled vision of the very young. Here the child's-eye-view of the opening underlines the ironies of the ending. Agnes, Anna's young half sister, likes both men, but she sees Mynors as "perfect," while Willie "made her feel towards him as she felt towards her doll when she happened to find it 'lying neglected on the floor.'"[17] Her opinion is not essentially departed from as the narrative unfolds the characters of the two men. Mynor's many "perfections" are made apparent, while Willie's awkward diffidence and clumsy movements are equally emphasized and allowed to cloud his merits in the eyes of his society. The conclusion leaves the perfect Mynors in ascendance, while Willie's body lies like a discarded and forgotten rag doll at the bottom of a pit-shaft.

Anna, who, in the beginning of her relationship with Mynors, looks upon him as Agnes does (69), and feels the motherly emotion toward Willie that Agnes feels (10), ends by marrying Mynors knowing she can never feel passionately for him in spite of his excellences, and believing that her deepest feeling will always be for Willie. Only at the end does she recognize that her maternal instincts toward him were part of her complete love for him, and she recognizes also that the knowledge has come too late. Her support in her marriage of duty is her certainty that Willie is doing well in Australia, boosted initially by the one hundred pounds she had given him on the day of his supposed departure. But Willie commits suicide instead. This triangle of relationships ends in the traditional sentimental comic pattern of a wedding for the heroine, but the absurdities inherent in the conclusion bring it nearer the tragicomic anomalies of life.

Another image used in the introduction of a character and recurring significantly throughout the tale is the nun-like nature of Anna. In the beginning it is the stateliness and quietude of her appearance that calls forth the comparison (7-8). But as her history is told, one sees that the extreme discipline of her homelife (40-41) has created a habit of mind that makes the epithet of "nun-like" more deeply descriptive.

There are ironies involved in the use of this image. Anna has the intelligence and imagination to question the more garish aspects of the Wesleyan-Methodist religion practiced in the Potteries. Yet the religious mores of her society cause her considerable anguish when she finds that she cannot accept them. The image of a nun, with its connotations of implicit faith and dogged obedience, emphasizes the irony of the position of the questioning, rebellious Anna. In the light of this image, her marriage can be viewed as the substitution of her husband's system of authority over her for her father's system, and the former is of her own choosing, for she voluntarily gives all of her financial affairs, and even her personal bank-book, to Mynors to control. She renounces her freedom on the financial side because she recognizes that she is doubly bound on the emotional and social levels. When, after failing to be "converted" at the revival, she carries out the irksome duty of visiting the homes of her backsliding pupils of the Sunday School with "the cold, fierce joy of the nun in her penance" (79-80), so, after failing to recognize in time where her instincts for love really lay, she determines, in the same vein, to devote her life to being a good wife to Mynors.

A second triangle of relationships intimately connected with that of the Anna-Mynors-Willie triangle, is the one made up of Anna, her father, and Mrs. Sutton, the benevolent, active churchwoman who is a member of the second family of Bursley society. Bennett draws the links close. Mrs. Sutton is a relative of Mynors and an old "flame" (193) of Ephraim. Mrs. Sutton is crucially involved in Anna's affairs from her twenty-first birthday onward. She favors Anna's connection with Mynors and takes steps to promote it. Her kind, mothering ways strongly draw Anna to her, while her great religious faith brings Anna's spiritual problem to a crisis. It is through Mrs. Sutton that Anna is taken on holiday to the Isle of Man where Mynors proposes to her. Mrs. Sutton's daughter, Beatrice, influences Anna, indirectly, to use money for her traveling clothes which her father had refused to give her. Later, the Suttons' notions of her trousseau needs cause Anna to demand money from her father in words that stir his final renunciation of any ties with her. Finally, a promissory note owned by the old miser, that was forged by Willie in Mr. Sutton's name, is stolen by Anna from her father and burnt. Anna's action helps to break down Willie's morale.

The interconnectedness of characters and events makes it possible for Bennett to represent clearly the pressures exerted by each person on the other in a small community, the burdens of their heritage, and the crippling aspects developed, as a result, in each personality. His use of advanced psychological theory appears in his treatment of almost all the major figures. Certainly, in Anna and in Ephraim, one can see, beyond the consistency that gives them individuality, the contradictions in their beings which give rise to many of the absurdities of the human condition. This was avant-garde thinking in Bennett's day as Lafourcade has observed.[18] Bennett does not carry his examination of the crushingly absurd as far in *Anna* as he does in some of his later novels, yet the level achieved gives a very moving statement of the power, but lack of point, of the illusions upon which societies are structured.

In choosing Anna as heroine and her father as antagonist in the story, Bennett begins a theme that is examined in many of his later books. The struggle between generations, with its timeworn but necessary conclusion for each generation, is given careful and moving treatment, reaching profundity in *The Old Wives' Tale*. In *Anna* the strife is short. The parental shackles are thrust off, but only thrust off in part, for they are also withdrawn. Anna's rebellious bid for freedom is accompanied by sorrow for her father's turning from her, and fear that she cannot stand alone. The shackles are then merely transferred.

In Bennett's honest statement of the *Five Towns* tale, however, he can depict the pathetic waste of imaginative and emotional potential in the choice Anna makes, but at the same time suggest the irony that, given her temperament, had she chosen the other road, her potentialities might still not have been developed. Willie's weakness might not have satisfied her independent soul either. In the intensity of the moment of recognizing their mutual love she is not moved to murmur a word of endearment, but whispers softly the exhortation: "Be a man" (358). Willie's response is not to make one last effort to succeed by going to a new society in Australia, but to opt out of all society by committing a suicide that will not be discovered.

The conclusion leaves Anna isolated from love. The responsibility for this futile waste of a powerful human resource is shown to lie partly in individual weakness and partly in society's obtuseness. Anna will appear to her society as the successful, happy matron. And her appearance will help to preserve the very standards by which her chance for fulfillment and happiness was destroyed.

This treatment of repression expresses Bennett's further consideration of the illusory in life. The irony inherent in the conclusion emphasizes Bennett's conception of the condition of life, but indicates his opinion that it need not be as it is. The conditions are man-made. They can be changed. He said of *Anna* that it is "tragic but not necessarily so."[19] Presumably, this statement can be related to the point just made, but it can also be related to the scale of suffering depicted in only one life. Walter Allen claims that in *Anna*, "for the first and only time in his life, Bennett was writing at the tragic level."[20] Vernon Pritchett claims that Bennett was not a tragic writer, but only a pathetic one.[21] It can be said that Bennett presents a conflict and a wastage of human resource which is tragic even on the individual level; but, since Anna's life is a representative ordinary life, the implications of conflict and wastage on a worldwide scale magnify the disaster. It cannot be considered merely pathetic. Pathos presupposes no struggle.

It is apparent that much of the life of Bursley is dominated by a strict Wesleyan Methodism which makes heavy demands on its adherents' time and money. It is the source of most of the social activity of the group of characters introduced, and, by its standards, they are confident in well-doing, as is Mynors, or are anguished over failures, as is Anna. Its black-and-white judgments create much of the repression that permeates life in the Five Towns.

Therefore, it is Titus Price who severely judges a child for stealing a Bible in Sunday School. Yet, pressed hard in his business, he embezzles Sunday School funds and approves his son's forgery. In his extremity, he does not seek mercy from his church, believing it would show no more mercy to him than he was willing to show to the young thief. The facade of his social pride will not allow him to beg either. He chooses to hang himself. It is Mynors's complacent attitude toward Willie's misfortunes, based upon the conviction that the sins of the fathers must fall upon the children, that closes Anna's heart to him. Carefully, Bennett reveals all the hypocrisy, sanctimoniousness, and cruelty that can flourish in a narrowly interpreted guide for conduct.

Bennett makes clear why a religion of this type would appeal to the Bursley populace. Most of them work long hours at some part of the pottery trade. His presentation of even the most minute aspect of the making of crockery (166-179) emphasizes the terrible monotony and seemingly unrelated activities of the masses employed in the different divisions of the works. The reduction of people to efficient machines, as seen in Mynors's plant, makes clear the habit of repression which dominates all their lives. Against the background of the smoking chimneys which choke Agnes's gilly-flowers and denude the countryside, and against the background of the stern, lifeless moralizing of the church, Anna's struggle to live fully comes to a speedy and inevitable close.

Bennett stresses the alienation from nature represented by Bursley society in his use of nature imagery. Only of the very young does he use images of the life and power stored in natural phenomena. As the narrative opens, the children freed from Sunday School rush "in two howling, impetuous streams, that widened, eddied, intermingled and formed backwaters." "She saw how miserably narrow, tepid and trickling the stream of her life had been, and had threatened to be. Now it gushed forth warm, impetuous, and full . . ." (36). When Bennett uses related imagery to describe an adult activity, it is with an irony that makes clear the aridity of the pursuit. Anna is ushered into the presence of the bank manager, and Bennett states: "Every Saturday morning he irrigated the whole town with fertilising gold" (52). In this way Bennett weaves carefully the details of his presentation into a close pattern that merges Anna's individual experience with every aspect of the total life of Bursley. And Bennett's comments radiate outward to encompass all industrialized civilization.

His comment is not simply condemnatory as his handling of the stream imagery may suggest. The ironies developed in the patterns

of descriptions are directly related to a rather long passage that
Bennett significantly placed in the first chapter and in which he
expatiates upon the necessarily incongruous activities of man. It
concludes: "Look down into the valley from this terrace-height
where love is kindling, embrace the whole smoke-girt amphithea-
tre in a glance. . . . On the one side is a wresting from nature's own
bowels of the means to waste her; on the other, an undismayed,
enduring fortitude. The grass grows: though it is not green, it
grows" (17-18). The unfolding of the story following this passage
demonstrates the truth of every aspect of the statement.

Bennett uses far less description in making personalities apparent in *Anna* than in *A Man*. He reveals character through speech
and action, his subtle use of humor providing the humanizing
element. This is most apparent in his treatment of Ephraim
Tellwright, who is far from being a simple "villain of the piece." In
chapter 2 the details of Tellwright's background stress his taciturni-
ty, his tyrannical treatment of his family, and his business acumen.
After he has impatiently knocked for entrance to his house while
Anna dawdled in the back garden, a brief dialogue ensues.
Expecting anger, Anna is astounded when the old man only says:
"Ye've been daydreaming eh, Sis?" In happy relief "she had a
fleeting wish to hug the tyrant" (37-38). A moving pathos is
indicated in the extent to which the emotions are stifled in this
family. Yet there is that which causes one to smile with the
pleasure of the love-starved girl gathering a crumb of human
communication in delighted surprise. The shrewdness and the
spark of sympathy, illuminated in the old man's character, go far
toward mitigating the effect of his severe eccentricities.

After Anna's introduction as the calm, stately, nun-like person
who habitually conceals her feelings beneath her ordered exterior,
Bennett proceeds to use every detail of the story to delineate
aspects of her nature voluntarily, or involuntarily, hidden, while
highlighting her father's attitudes. Like *A Man*, the unfolding
narrative reveals the growth of self-knowledge in the central
figure.

Revolutionary experiences come fast on the heels of her twenty-
first birthday. Not all of them can she meet with "the courage to
enjoy" (37). After her father makes her read the many lists of
shares now legally hers, she feels as if her "brain [were] a

menagerie of monstrous figures" (46). When she returns to her kitchen after nominally receiving her fifty thousand pounds, "she peeled the potatoes with more than her usual thrifty care; the peel so thin as to be transparent" (49). The images and actions are carefully chosen from the girl's everyday experience. Through them Bennett accurately catches acute psychological insights. The degree of her fear of her great wealth is gauged in the degree of thinness of the potato peelings. All of Bennett's facts are naturally placed, but selectively chosen, for purposes similar to the one discussed above.

A long description of Anna's kitchen reveals another method Bennett uses to elucidate her character. The effect is far from a dull catalog. All who visit the kitchen are impressed with the ordered, unhurried, timeless, careful existence that the room reflects. As such, it represents Anna, and the long line of women who had cared for it before her.

It is obvious that Bennett has full control of his material to shape its parts to tell the story he wishes told. All is done in the most unassuming prose style. Out of context almost any passage will lack the striking qualities readers vividly remember from writers like Conrad, Hudson, Hardy or even Galsworthy. But, as the tension of Anna's story mounts steadily, a passage concluding chapter 12 makes a powerful comment upon shackled lives: "The next day Sarah Bodrey died—she who had never lived save in the fetters of slavery and fanaticism. . . . The Priory, deserted, gave up its rickety furniture to a van from Hanbridge, where, in an auction-room, the frail sticks lost their identity in a medley of other sticks, and ceased to be. Then the bricklayer, the plasterer, the painter, and the paperhanger came to the Priory, and whistled and sang in it"(341). This passage reflects its own ironies upon the description in the first chapter already referred to. Man is forever at the mercy of his own inventions and conventions. His compromises continue his illusions and frequently destroy his spirit.

Excellent as the novel is, it is not flawless. Some episodes are developed to a length disproportionate to their value in the narrative. With too little point a chapter is devoted to Anna's visit to Mrs. Sutton's sewing meeting. Another episode not sufficiently integrated into the smooth flow of the narrative is Anna's visit to Mynors's works. The style changes as a lengthy documentary account of the development of the potter's craft is given. More could have been done to develop Willie's and Mynors's characters in order to give greater understanding of Anna's falling in love with Willie and to make more tenable the ironies involved in her final choice of Mynors. However, these weaknesses cannot detract from the judgment that in writing *Anna* Bennett became a novelist of note.

Chapter Three

Extremes in Experimentation and Manipulation of Old Formulas

Having discovered what he could do in the varying types of his first five novels, Bennett's desire to work became insatiable, his capacity phenomenal. Within the next seven years he produced ten novels, an autobiographical account, a guide for young writers, two collections of short stories; he began three long series of essays and articles for weeklies; he collaborated in the writing of four plays; he traveled; he moved residence frequently; he increased his voluminous correspondence. The novels crammed into this period of frenetic activity include: two serious studies of women, *Leonora* (1903) and *Sacred and Profane Love* (1905); two lighthearted narratives of men, *A Great Man* (1904) and *Hugo* (1906); a variation of the humorous detective story, *Teresa of Watling Street* (1904); one serious study of divorce, *Whom God Hath Joined* (1906); two humorous melodramas, *The Sinews of War* (1906) and *The City of Pleasure* (1907); one non-humorous melodrama, *The Statue* (1908); and one "idyllic diversion," *Helen with The High Hand* (1910)—a humorous treatment of miserliness foiled. Bennett's flamboyance, his extremes in experimentation, his manipulation of old formulas, are particularly noticeable in this group. And varying humor characterizes most of them.

Teresa of Watling Street

Coming to *Teresa of Watling Street* from *Anna of the Five Towns,* a reader would not hesitate to agree with Bennett when he abjured H. G. Wells to "ignore my next book. It is naught."[1] He tried to prevent the serial being published in book form by Chatto and

Windus,[2] but failed. He wrote to E. V. Lucas in 1924: "I always regard *Teresa* as the world's worst novel."[3] His assessment will not be modified here.

In the novel Bennett presents Raphael Craig, manager of a suburban bank who is slowly disposing of thousands of gold sovereigns to wreak vengeance upon his enemy, Simon Locke, a director of Craig's bank and a magnate in the city. However, Craig's intrigue does not take place in the foreground of the tale. It is made the mysterious background movement against which the young amateur detective, Redgrave, pits his talents for sleuthing. In the foreground with Redgrave are Craig's adopted twin daughters, Juana and Teresa, and the Scotland Yard detective, Nolan, disguised as the Craig's man-of-all-work, Mike. Bennett appears to aim at doing for the banking business what he had done for the hotel business in *The Grand Babylon Hotel.* But he fails to produce anything to compare with the attractive balance of humor and high adventure in the earlier novel. Because the details of Craig's vendetta are not presented until Craig's explanation in the penultimate chapter, a brooding quality is given to the novel which permeates all the preceding chapters and prevents the humor associated with Redgrave's sleuthing activities from creating any effect except that of being extraneous.

Lenora

After Bennett's treatment of repression in *Anna of the Five Towns* he had begun to think of Anna's opposite and develop the traits of the more emancipated woman. In *Lenora* Bennett examines a short period in the life of the forty-year-old Leonora Stanway. Other important figures are: her husband, John Stanway; their daughters, Ethel, Rose and Milly; Arthur Twemlow, Stanway's former partner; and Uncle Meshach, Stanway's relative. Dain, Stanway's solicitor; Fred Ryley, Ethel's boyfriend; Harry Burgess, Milly's friend; and Aunt Hannah, Meshach's sister, complete the list of important characters.

The omniscient narrator's inclusions blend with Leonora's thoughts to give the effect of almost constant meditation. Arthur Twemlow after twenty-five years' absence disrupts the dreaming monotony of Leonora's life, brings her husband's business affairs to a crisis, and affects the careers of each of the three daughters. The result of Uncle Meshach's desire for justice for Twemlow, while ignorant of his nephew's financial plight, is that John Stanway commits suicide, Leonora is free to marry Twemlow who loves her and with whom she has fallen in love, and her three daughters can follow their individual ambitions freed from the domination of their Victorian father.

There are twelve chapters in the novel. In the first Leonora's state of mind is presented in description capturing her day-dreaming memories. But her relationship to her three daughters is presented in effective dialogue. Then, in direct contrast to a passage emphasizing the mysteries of the wisdom of old age as seen in Meshach, is placed a passage interweaving the thoughtless, carefree nature of young Millicent. Both are foils for the middle-aged Leonora who feels she has already gained much of the insight of old Meshach while preserving much of the spirit and longings of Millicent.

The chapter also presents a view of Stanway in the midst of his four women, lacking understanding of each and only able to preserve a feeling of his close relationship through his demonstra-tions of authority over them. All his women preserve to Stanway the appearance of obedience, but in private an independence and a power to manipulate are asserted. The grounds for Leonora's belief that her life is over are made clear through her recognition of her place in her husband's life and in the disobedience of her daughters which marks the first break in the bonds that held them to her.

Chapter 2 concentrates upon the part played by Uncle Meshach through chance and intent to bring about a resolution in Leonora's affairs. His representation as an ancient who has virtually opted out of life to watch it more clearly from the sidelines is drawn to the point of caricature. Bennett demonstrates that the "wisdom" of age, when divorced from the facts and used by a radical eccentric, results in ends unforeseen and frequently disastrous. By the end of chapter 2, Bennett has generated two movements: Leonora's search for fulfillment and Twemlow's desire to have justice done. These two movements are in opposition and provide the only tension in the narrative.

From this point ten chapters trace the loosing of Leonora's hold on each member of her family through death or the independence conferred upon them by marriage and the accomplishment of isolating ambitions. These chapters also trace the gradual growth of a new affection for Arthur Twemlow and the transferral of her dependence to him. The reciprocal effects of her awareness that the inevitable loss of some of her emotional ties is causing a reaching out for a substitute, and of her gradual realization that a substitute allows her to loosen her hold upon her daughters, is very carefully and subtly drawn by Bennett.

Through Bennett's arrangement of his material comes, with a sincerity that is considerably moving, his recognition of the dichotomy between flesh and spirit which constitutes the problem of human existence. And he presents the strictures of society which have developed to coincide with the aging of the body regardless of the state of the animating spirit. Leonora's longing to live youthfully, and her belief that at forty her life is over, form the crux of the novel. Bennett demonstrates the ambiguities of her situation. Then, he gives his presentation a conclusion that draws all the ambiguities together, but does not resolve them.

It becomes increasingly clear that any strength the work possesses must rest upon Bennett's treatment of the character of Leonora. She is introduced as presenting to the public "her customary air of haughty and rapt leisure."[4] Clay-soiled girls watch her pass in the September sunshine. The descriptive passage (3-4) is significant in interpreting the meanings to be drawn from Leonora's story. Direct mention of "September sunshine" is the first indication that Leonora is entering the autumn of her life. It is the eve of her fortieth birthday. Beginning her story in early autumn, Bennett follows the events of two years to the summer season in which Leonora begins a new life with Arthur Twemlow. Between are the winter death of Aunt Hannah and the financial crisis this precipitates, the spring suicide of John Stanway, the summer courtship of Ethel, the long winter of Leonora's denial of her love, the spring launching of her three daughters in their respective careers, the return of Arthur Twemlow and the resolution of their affair in a summer marriage.

It is not by chance that in the autumn of her life Leonora, married, with grown daughters, experiences her first deep love for a man. It is not by chance that in the season of new life and fresh beginnings John Stanway destroys himself. The one capable of new growth is given the opportunity for it; the other, proven incapable of learning from past folly, is stricken. That Leonora vacillates initially, then takes the opportunity without its making any vital change within her, gives point to the irony. Leonora lacks will, just as Anna lacked will. Where Anna could not follow the dictates of her heart, Leonora can and does. Yet some indication of promise unrealized is left with the reader. In the last chapter is the following statement: "And revelling in the self-confidence and the masterful ascendancy which underlay Arthur's usual reticent demeanor, she resumed with exquisite relief her natural supineness. She began to depend on him"(361). Leonora's autumn has only taken on the appearance of an Indian summer.

Through the text Bennett has repeated the use of the word *illusion* and depicted illusory conceptions and situations with such frequency as to appear almost too insistent. Yet his point has been missed by readers who complain about a contrived happy ending. Leonora's second chance for happiness is as much fraught with illusion as the many specific illusions cited throughout the text. The opening sentence of the last chapter indicates this: "The last day of the dramatic portion of Leonora's life was that on which she went to London with Milly" (339). This statement precedes the resolution of her affair with Twemlow and can be taken as a comment upon it. At the end of the story there has been a change of state, but essentially no change in her behavior. There is, then, no guarantee within the story that Leonora will be any happier in the future than the irreconcilables of her nature can allow her to be.

Bennett had shown in *Anna* the power of an adverse environment over the individual, while in Leonora he demonstrates the power of hereditary tendencies to negate an apparently advantageous situation. The result in the second study is to reduce the degree of importance of the heroine's problem and the emotional involvement of the reader in it. Anna, although pressured, does make a choice; Leonora merely drifts. It remained for Bennett to show a woman who makes her own freedoms and acts fully in them. This he attempted in *Sacred and Profane Love*.

A Great Man and *Hugo*

Bennett's eighth novel, *A Great Man*, is different in kind from its seven forerunners. Its subtitle and its dedication imply both the approach and the content to be expected. The subtitle calls the work "A Frolic"; the dedication presents the work to Bennett's "dear friend Frederick Marriott and to the imperishable memory of old times." Obviously a lighthearted recollection of the period of Bennett's initiation into the world of authors is indicated. A brief synopsis of the story verifies this surmise.

The novel opens at the birth of Henry Shakspere (*sic*) Knight . The first six chapters present humorous incidents of his childhood. Then, the hero in his twenty-third year writes a story that is accepted for publication. All the experiences of an instant success are humorously delineated: his first crushing reviews by critics, his first interview for a woman's weekly, the unwelcome glare of publicity over his actions, his first society party, his acceptance of his new wealth and position, his marriage to his first interviewer, and, finally, his succumbing to the notion that his popular novels are great literature and that he is indeed an important man.

Bennett did not advance his techniques by writing *A Great Man,* but he demonstrated the slickness with which he could turn them to use. His comic lists, comic alliterations, humorous situations, ironic innuendoes, have all appeared in his earlier books. However, the raillery complemented by sympathy, which is the main source of pleasure in the book, he was to use with greater success in later works such as *Buried Alive* (1908) and *The Card* (1911). As he said of the book to H. G. Wells: "having conceived it as a 'lark', I fell into the error of regarding it technically as a 'lark' also."[5] He intended in his next novel, *Hugo,* to pay much more attention to technique, but dashed off the novel in only three weeks.

Hugo, a middle-aged bachelor and owner of a department store, is infatuated with one of his employees, Camilla Payne. He discovers she has been involved with his half brother Louis Ravengar and is involved with Francis Tudor, a wealthy tenant in one of Hugo's flats. Ravengar is a madman who means to marry Camilla or prevent her marrying anyone else. Tudor tries to protect Camilla by arranging a simulated burial for her, but he dies suddenly before this is accomplished, while Camilla is drugged and kidnapped by Ravengar who means to bury her indeed. Hugo, suspicious of his half brother from the beginning, manages to follow clues to a graveyard where he saves the girl. The melodrama has some effective moments and includes some ingenious comedy but it is not the whimsical combination of those elements that is found in *The Grand Babylon Hotel.*

At two points in the narrative Bennett has his characters make statements that relate to ideas developed in *Sacred and Profane Love,* the next novel to be discussed here. Ravengar says: "You ought to pity me. Did I choose my temperament, my individuality? As I am, so I was born, and from his character no man can escape".[6] Francis Tudor speaks from his recording: "But in love there isn't often any question of right. Human instincts have no regard for human justice, and when the instinct is strong enough, the sense of justice simply ceases to exist for it"(210). These ideas are not developed in *Hugo,* but find exemplification in the character and behavior of Carlotta Peel.

Sacred and Profane Love

Bennett had high hopes for this third study of female behavior. *Sacred and Profane Love* was to explore the character of a woman of "genius"[7] who chose to break away from all conventional sexual restraints. This conception of the central figure, and the choice of first person narration, subjects the reader to a somewhat hysterical account. However, when H. G. Wells strongly criticized it, Bennett defended the novel: "All I would calim for Carlotta is that now & then she does what a real woman would do. . . . Again, I must agree with you as to the style. But incidentally you must remember that this is not my style, but Carlotta's style, & that it cost me a Hades of a lot of trouble."[8]

From an account of events, the novel would appear to be a melodramatic romance of the Ouida type.[9] There are, in fact, all the ingredients of a popular sensational novel with extra touches of the "bawdy."[10] However, it is not a sentimental tear-jerker. And Bennett included it among his serious works, indicating this by the subtitle, "A Novel in Three Episodes." It is repudiated by Walter Allen as "almost the most tasteless novel ever written by a major novelist."[11] It is described by James Hall as "a complete failure."[12] Yet the novel offers interesting evidence of Bennett's endeavor to experiment with form in an attempt to advance his technique in preparation for writing the masterpiece he had long been contemplating.[13]

Divided into three parts, Carlotta's story covers a period of ten years within which the events form a patterned cycle. In part 1, on the eve of her twenty-first birthday, she first experiences sexual passion. On her birthday her aunt dies. The emancipated girl takes her inheritance, goes to London where her first novel is published, and is soon in love with her publisher. In part 2, after five years, she holds successful salons, but plans to cast aside her London life in an attempt to have some more permanent basis for her love. Following their third encounter when they planned to live together, all is disrupted with the double suicide of the publisher and his wife. Part 3, after another five years, brings Carlotta to the restoration of her first love. She describes five encounters with Diaz: sighting him at a sidewalk cafe and helping him home; next evening when he shouts at her in a drunken rage; next morning agreeing to retire with him to Fontainebleau; a year later giving him a libretto she had written for him; finally, attending the performance of the opera he wrote. The symmetrically increasing numbers indicate the direction and the degree in which the tension is meant to develop.

Death attends each of Carlotta's great moments of happiness. The single death of her aunt precipitates her into London life after her sexual initiation with Diaz; the double suicide of her lover and his wife leaves her a lonely wanderer; then follows her own death immediately after she senses that her mission has been achieved with Diaz's successful return to the world of music. When she is most ecstatic her position is most equivocal. She grasps after a level of emotional experience that she desperately wants to prolong, but that from its very nature is the most ephemeral.

Carlotta never becomes a prostitute, nor is she promiscuous, but she never marries. In the end she has only completely loved one man. She spent one night with him at the beginning of their relationship and one year with him at the end. This presentation of a woman who chooses to cultivate her sensuous nature and follow her instincts wherever they lead her is described by Bennett as "spiritually expensive."[14] He did not wish to write much in that vein.[15] Nevertheless, he never repudiated the book. He called it a "tour de force,"[16] but recommended it among his best books to a discriminating reader.[17] The obviousness in the stylization of the material reveals an arbitrariness in Bennett's choice rather than the natural development of a form to meet the demands of the nature of the story.

Bennett had used first-person narration in the short story that is probably the forerunner of *Sacred and Profane Love*.[18] Seventeen years later Bennett highly admired the technique James Joyce used in Molly Bloom's famous monologue at the end of *Ulysses*—a monologue which reveals much more intimate matter much more frankly, but without causing the reader discomposure. Bennett called the passage "immortal."[19] However, his desire to follow traditional methods of presentation, and his conception of his heroine, made it impossible for him to approach the later success of Joyce. Nevertheless, at least one of the cultivated readers of the novel found it almost incredible that Bennett could show the knowledge of a woman's nature that the novel contained for her.[20] Perhaps the problem lies in the fact that Bennett made a mistake in taste by attempting to be *comme trop vrai*; he did not use the discretion he so much admired in the de Goncourts.[21]

The ambiguities worked into the texture of the novel must be taken into account before any final judgment can be made about the value of Carlotta's story. Each of the critics cited above, who found the narrative so distasteful, has taken Carlotta's tale as she tells it, at its maudlin surface level, and dismissed it. However, Bennett includes many ironies that must modify any conclusions drawn only from the surface.

The remembered incidents and reactions are given sometimes as dramatized present occurrences, sometimes as remembered descriptions. When dramatized, they are likely to be taken at face value; when described, they are more likely to be questioned. It becomes clear gradually that Carlotta is necessarily giving a one-sided point of view and that at least one other point of view is possible from the facts. Also, there is the interesting possibility that Carlotta, at the end, may have been consciously trying to convince herself that the facts were not as they were, but as she would have had them be. The obvious complexities involved in the development of this novel would appear to make it Bennett's most ambitious effort thus far. But the realization falls far short of the possibilities.

The City of Pleasure, The Sinews of War

Following *Sacred and Profane Love,* Bennett returned in both *The City of Pleasure*[22] and *The Sinews of War*[23] to narratives that combine almost all of the possible elements of melodrama with Bennett's special brand of humor for his serials. *The City of Pleasure* has an entrepreneur as hero; it has a disappearing body, a robbery, an abduction, attempted murder by shooting and poisoning, mistaken identity, twin sisters for romantic interest, fairground activities for gusto, and multiple marriages at the end. *The Sinews of War* includes most of these, but adds pursuit by sea to a tropic isle and buried Russian treasure. Obviously, these novels require no further discussion here.

Whom God Hath Joined

In *Whom God Hath Joined*[24] Bennett presents the difficulties within two marriages which bring each couple into the divorce court. The novel opens with Lawrence Ridware's problem at the point where he has discovered his wife's infidelity and wishes to take some definite action. His brother, Mark, summoned from London, insists that the matter be brought to court. Lawrence, a legal clerk, determines to have Charles Fearns, the head of his firm, take charge of his case, but discovers that Fearns disapproves of his proposed action.

Fearns's reluctance lies in his history of philandering and his fears that one day his wife will bear it no longer. Lawrence's case is given to a junior member of the firm. It is proceeding swiftly, when two events occur that radically alter the immediate course of the lives of the two men. Charles Fearns commits adultery with his children's governess while his wife is away, and the fact is discovered by his twenty-one-year-old daughter, Annunciata, whose utter innocence of the way of the world has been assiduously protected. And Phyllis Ridware's lover, Emery Greatbatch, dies suddenly before their case has come to trial.

The result of the first event is that Charles Fearns's home is abandoned by his family and he is precipitated into the divorce court; the result of the second event is that Phyllis, in the bitterness of her loss, reveals the fact that Lawrence was illegitimately born in Scotland and this enables the judge to dismiss the case on a question of domicile. When Fearns's case comes to trial, it is dropped because his daughter cannot bring herself to testify against her father. After a period of suffering for both men, their lives return to the general contours of their earlier existences: Lawrence Ridware, divorced, lives down his notoriety and engrosses himself in his books, his substitute for human relationships, and

Charles Fearns is accepted back by his wife, although they move to a neighboring town where it is soon rumored that Charles is philandering again.

This synopsis emphasizes that Bennett's concern in its construction is to reveal the difficulties created by personality—clashes within the intimacy of family life—and to show how these natural difficulties are increased to destructive levels when they involve recourse to the court. The arbitrariness of the law due to its mechanical operation, and its possible manipulation, demonstrate the contraries that exist in the human psyche and that underlie and weaken the foundation of all systems man has built.

Those readers who interpret the novel as didactic, damning the process of the law and of divorce laws in particular, do not note that Bennett said he "never had the slightest intention of making the book 'propagandist'," [25] and they do not note accurately where Bennett's emphasis lies. The ironies in the male-versus-female problem are more sharply demonstrated through difficulties involved in the operation of the law. A lawyer, who seeks help in his personal problem from the fallible courts of law, without first examining all the facts which the court will make public, is asking for trouble. As Bennett constructs the story, the man whose case is not brought to judgment by law is the man who is happiest as the novel ends. The solutions for his characters lie outside the arbitrary forms by which man has bound himself.

Bennett sets the struggle of his seven characters in the Five Towns district and opens the novel with a panoramic view of the area taken from the vantage point of Toft End in Bursley. The long descriptive passage with cumulative significance is a technique Bennett has used effectively before in *Anna*. From viewing the panorama of the countryside and gaining an all-embracing sympathetic viewpoint, the reader must focus upon Lawrence Ridware struggling uphill from the suburb of Bleakridge. The choice of language and arrangement of words make his introduction ironic. The opening note of loving comprehension is to be balanced with the detachment that the ironic viewpoint gives. With Ridware's story, we descend from the heights where the comprehensive view is possible and follow the course of events on the levels of the valley where judgment becomes limited and questionable.

The approach is mainly from Lawrence's point of view. Glimpses of Charles Fearns and brief references to his daughter and wife are placed at significant intervals in the first two chapters which establish Ridware's situation. The following four chapters mainly develop the Fearnses' affairs. Chapter 3 introduces Annunciata. Bennett sensitively captures the nature of this innocent, pampered girl, who fortuitously assumes the burdens of housekeeping for a day; and he accurately registers the shock she receives when faced that night with the fact of her father's infidelity to her mother. Bennett's rapport with the young enables him to achieve a delicacy of treatment which makes the girl appealing.

Bennett has accurately gauged the extent to which he needed to develop in the reader an awareness of the temperaments and emotional states of both Lawrence Ridware and Annunciata Fearns. More than a third of the novel has been taken to establish their limited but sensitive natures and to register the degree of the shocks sustained by each. This detailed background enables the reader to appreciate fully, after the course of events is narrated, the poignancy of the association of these people at the end of the novel, whose names were maliciously linked in the opening chapters, but who remain arbitrarily worlds apart.

Chapters 4, 5, and 6 develop the impact of the discovery upon each of the principal people involved. This group of chapters brings both Lawrence Ridware and Charles Fearns to the contemplation of virtually uninhabitable homes and shows the relationship between the crisis in Ridware's life and the developing crisis in Fearns's. The novel comes to its midpoint where all its major figures are suffering and where all look to the one source to achieve an end to their unhappiness.

In chapters 7 and 8, Bennett brings Phyllis's situation forward. He makes poignant the desperation of a woman who had regained the love her youthful stubbornness had cost her, but who now must suffer its irremediable loss. Bennett does not sentimentalize, but makes vividly concrete Phyllis's situation in her clutching fingers sensing the more lasting texture of the doomed man's jacket.

Chapters 9, 10, and 11 bring the issues in the cases of the Ridwares and the Fearnses to their crises in the courts. The penultimate chapter presents Annunciata and her mother preparing to journey to London for the trial. They are observed by the porter and male commuters whose feelings indicate the double standard of morality that has brought these women to their unenviable position. Also clearly indicated is the utterly false attitude that Annunciata has cultivated against her father and her equally false view of the court.

The final chapter reviews the situation of the principal characters some three years after their trials. Bennett dismisses Phyllis Ridware with the statement that she has disappeared in London. Lawrence's cousin, Sarah, is dying and requires a nurse. Annunciata Fearns is sent to him. Lawrence reflects upon the attraction she had held for him for years, but he refuses to let desire stir the calm of his present existence and the placidity of hers. The contours of the story make Lawrence's pessimistic conclusion questionable.

As in *Anna*, so in *Whom God Hath Joined*, Bennett has presented the woeful waste of human resources in crippled lives. However, the effect lacks the power Bennett achieved in *Anna*. Although the two divorce affairs are essentially linked at numerous points, the fact that there is more than one center of interest diffuses the power. Five characters vie for interest in *Whom God Hath Joined*, and none of them is revealed to the extent that Anna is. The reader watches Anna struggle hard to overcome the coils that bind her, and her situation provides her with an opportunity to act heroically. But in *Whom God Hath Joined* few of the characters struggle or are moved to an unselfish consideration of another; all the characters but Annunciata are bent on achieving small selfish satisfactions, and even Annunciata's aims are distorted with a youthful fanaticism.

But admirable characters are not necessary to artistic success. Bennett succeeds in making the miser, Henry Earlforward, in *Riceyman Steps* (1923) mean much more to the reader than any of the characters of *Whom God Hath Joined*. The problem in the latter is indicated in the final paragraph of the long opening passage. Bennett there indicates what becomes in the course of the narrative the overbearing presence of the omniscient narrator. The machinery for viewing the characters is too obvious; the characters are too obviously exhibited. The ironies woven into the tale to preserve a balance from the sentimentality which hovers over the opening viewpoint too often isolate the reader into mockery rather than invite him to smile wryly upon recognizing a constant human foible. Bennett criticized *Whom God Hath Joined*, some months after its publication, as "a clumsy book," adding "but not dull."[26]

Whom God Hath Joined was an ambitious effort. His attempt to interweave more than one serious plot-line, his use of the devices at his command to produce a greater density of texture, his more prominent use of comic techniques, his effort to achieve "nobility,"[27] all show the way in which he hoped to develop. That he had not mastered a synthesis of these techniques is clear.

Helen with the High Hand and *The Statue*

Before Bennett collaborated with Eden Phillpotts for the second time in producing *The Statue* (1908), he speedily wrote *Helen with The High Hand* (1910)[28] subtitled "An Idyllic Diversion." It is set in the Five Towns and features two major characters, James Ollerenshaw and his step-grandniece Helen Rathbone. In the group of the fantasias *Helen with the High Hand* is different because Bennett chooses for the first time[29] in his novels to turn a wholly humorous gaze upon the inhabitants of his birthplace, and he selects not a young, feckless hero, but a sixty-four-year-old shrewd Bursley businessman. He is alienated from Helen's mother and scarcely knows his step-grandniece. Old James is no match for Helen's wiles in getting him suddenly to spend money in a manner inconceivable before her advent into his home.

The conflict between the superficially reluctant, gruff old man who secretly learns to enjoy luxurious living and the determined, wily young woman who combines good nature with archness is the source of much typical Bennett humor. However, Bennett intends that his treatment of this particular narrative will not be considered "playing down" to the public in the manner condemned in *The City of Pleasure*.[30] He does not caricature his characters; they are believable. With the simple plot-line, Bennett is free to expend his energies on the presentation of some of the abundance of humorous incidents well known to him in the rich comedy of manners of his Five Towns people.

Very little need be said about *The Statue* (1908).[31] Courlander, the millionaire owner of an estate bearing a frighteningly large statue, has a son who loves and secretly marries the daughter of Crampiron, his millionaire rival. The contest between the fathers disrupts the marriage of their offspring. When a financial crisis develops causing the opposition of the older men to increase to a hatred that ends in Crampiron killing Courlander, the separation of the young couple appears to be permanent, as Maurice, the son, seeks to revenge his father's death and repudiates the daughter of his father's murderer. Eventually, the mysterious statue is revealed to be a radio tower by which financial transactions were secretly sent to Europe. This is dismantled. Crampiron explains the manslaughter to his son-in-law Maurice; the older man is spirited away to Algiers to spend the rest of his life in exile, and his daughter is restored to her husband.

This account indicates that the plot provides the usual high adventure of Bennett's serials, but it is given far less fairy-tale action and much more effective mystery and detective work. The intrigue is soundly based in political maneuvers, and the displays of wealth and social glamor are appropriately drawn. Bennett weaves his typical ironies throughout the novel. Altogether, one can conclude that there are less of the faults of the earlier serials and more of competent journalism. Bennett considered this novel "on [its] plane, sound and conscientious work."[32] However, the expectations of readers familiar with Bennett's better books find no satisfaction in merely competent journalism, in extremes in experimentation, or in slick manipulation of old formulas.

Chapter Four
A Double Triumph

At thirty-nine Bennett entered a decisive period in his life. In an exciting year and a half he planned to marry one woman but, rebuffed, he married another. Within three months of his marriage he began to write *The Old Wives' Tale* (1908) which, after two months' work upon it, he interrupted to write in the following two months, *Buried Alive* (1908); then he returned to *The Old Wives' Tale* to finish it within six months, and both books were published before the year ended.

During these months he also had published his melodramas: *The Ghost*, *The City of Pleasure*, and *The Statue*; his pocket philosophies: *The Reasonable Life* and *How to Live on Twenty-Four Hours a Day*; *The Human Machine*, a collection of articles previously published in *T. P.'s Weekly*; *The Grim Smile of the Five Towns*, a collection of short stories; *Things Which Have Interested Me, Third Series*. He dramatized *Anna of the Five Towns* under the title *Cupid and Commonsense*;[1] it was produced by the Stage Society at the Shaftesbury Theatre and required his presence in England for rehearsals. He collaborated with Phillpotts on another play, *The Sole Survivors*, which was never published or produced. And he began a series of articles in the *New Age* entitled "Books and Persons" under the pseudonym Jacob Tonson. He took holidays in San Remo and did a cycling tour of France. When one considers that, in the midst of all this activity, he had decided to put his hobby of fine calligraphy and illumination to special use, and set himself to write his first and only manuscript of *The Old Wives' Tale*, with astonishingly few errors or second choices,[2] one can only stand in awe of the discipline to which he subjected himself, not, it must be suspected, without great cost. Nevertheless, Bennett's astounding fecundity in this period is distinguished by its quality.

Buried Alive

Bennett combines in *Buried Alive* the vivacious humor which characterized *The Grand Babylon Hotel*, the sympathy with which he treated Henry Knight in *A Great Man*, the acute irony which distinguished *A Man From the North* and *Anna of the Five Towns*, and the craftsmanship heretofore reserved for his serious works.

The novel presents the experiences of the forty-year-old artist Priam Farll after the death of his valet, Henry Leek. Farll, a pathologically shy man, has used his valet as his buffer before the world. He cares nothing for the fame his paintings have attached to his name and has successfully avoided the limelight to the extent that no one knows what he looks like. When he is mistaken for his own valet and the dead valet is taken to be him, he has the wild notion of letting Leek be buried under his name, while he continues joyously unknown.

He is soon involved in problems of which he could not have conceived. In assuming Leek's identity, he acquires Leek's past, out of which emerges Alice Challice, a middle-aged Putney housekeeper of small means who sought a husband through a marriage bureau and caught Leek. Since Leek had sent Farll's picture as enticement, Alice pursues Farll. Out of the past also comes Leek's first wife and three lumbering sons, who briefly terrify the meek Farll.

At the same time Farll experiences the nation's mourning for his death. His astonishment and gratification send him to view his own funeral and interment with the full panoply of state honor in Westminster Abbey. Meanwhile, having married Alice and settled into a comfortable routine, he discovers that they need funds and he has only one means of earning money. He paints again, and through his painting is found out. A trial ensues which ends with Farll being proved to be Farll.

Bennett enjoys all the opportunities this story gives him to jibe at social groups, institutions, and organizations that restrict individual behavior according to preconceived notions of what is appropriate to great art and great artists. He enjoys contrasting the values of a simple life with those false values often attached to great wealth. He weaves into his account little vignettes of those who are neither simple nor wealthy, but who would use the simple and parasitically pander to the powerful. He joyously jabs the press, the courts, the nobility. And, over all, he shapes the framework of the idyllic love story of an incongruous pair at an awkward age. It was ambitiously conceived and cleverly achieved.

As the novel develops, from the caricature of a "type," Priam Farll grows into a multifaceted individual who wins the reader's amused sympathy. As the consequences of his mistaken identity begin to overtake him, his reactions are drawn by Bennett in such a manner that they seem to be accurate transcriptions of a living man. Bennett draws more delicately the simple, warm, motherly nature of the woman Farll comes to adore. He succeeds in sympathetically presenting Alice's utter lack of artistic judgment, her certainty that the evidence of her husband's genius is the sure sign of his lunacy, her overwhelming love for her afflicted husband, and her determination to shield him from all troubles. Her commonsense attitude to all things enables her to act with shrewdness and aplomb in the quite hilarious scene of the tea party at which the uninvited guests, Mrs. Leek and her three sons, first seek restitution of their rights and then leave, thankfully feeling they have avoided a liability.

The case of the American collector versus the English dealer duly comes before the court. Bennett's tracing of "the nation's curiosity" in this *cause celebre*, as fostered by the press, is equally hilarious. The trial resolves itself into a conflict between Farll's determination not to expose his neck with the two identifying moles, and the court's determination that somewhere in its corporate rules there must be the power to compel him to do so. Finally, the case is closed and Priam Farll, valuing his Alice more than ever, leaves England.

The novel is a tissue of familiar Bennett material. But there is nothing of the worn in his presentation. All is fresh, vital, and funny. As Wells wrote to Bennett: *"Buried Alive* is ripping good stuff. I have just been reading it. It's easy and skilful and humorous and daring and everything it ought to be."[3] Nothing in this novel fails to carry its full complement of comedy. Having thoroughly enjoyed himself and provided his readers with perhaps the best of his satiric comedies,[4] Bennett returned with increased artistic vigor to the writing of *The Old Wives' Tale*.

The Old Wives' Tale

Arnold Bennett began to write *The Old Wives' Tale* in the calm assurance that he had conceived a masterpiece. Following his usual practice, he had worked out the entire novel in his mind so that when he started to shape the fine script on the specially purchased paper, the words came in a steady flow of remarkable power. The steadiness of the flow, with Bennett's seeming surface simplicities, may lead the reader unfamiliar with Bennett's work to assume that he is being led into a plain narrative of dull lives. This impression should only be short-lived, if it is felt at all. As the steady stream with calm surface deceptively masks the relentless force that sweeps all before it, so Bennett's unadorned but carefully chosen prose, paragraph by paragraph, accumulates a strength that overwhelms the reader with the "terrible beauty which hides itself in the ugliness of life."[5] His massing of little insistent details, his "synthetic impressionism" creates a narrative of great complexity within unity.

In *The Old Wives' Tale* Bennett captures the impression of the passing of every day for a lifetime in the awareness of two average girls with their ordinary relatives and neighbors whose experiences encompass all those possible for the majority of mankind. Bennett's sympathetic persona gives a dimension to the experiences of these girls in which the reader feels profound truths have been imparted to him. It is certain that posterity will treasure *The Old Wives' Tale* as the classic Bennett believed it to be. What he had grasped in his consideration of existence, as did Henry James and Virginia Woolf, is that in the emotional lives of individuals the degree of comedy and the degree of tragedy are relative to their perceptions of experience.

Bennett marshals his material into four blocks. Book 1 presents the buoyant adolescence of the two sisters, Constance and Sophia Baines. They are superficially controlled by their impressive mother who cannot imagine the possibility of her girls harboring any thoughts but those she would have them think. The inherent rebelliousness of Sophia is carefully documented; the more docile nature of Constance is made clear. The dawning of romance in both girls is depicted; that of Sophia involving the death of her father and a runaway marriage; that of Constance involving the new direction of the shop and the removal of Mrs. Baines to her sister's home in Axe.

Book 2 follows Constance through her development as manager of her home, her adjustments to the facts of her marriage, her conception of a son, the deaths of her aunt and her mother. Samuel Povey, her husband, takes his place in the Bursley business district, cultivates the acquaintance of his cousin Daniel, takes up the cause of saving Daniel's life to the neglect of his health, and dies. The shop is bought by the elderly eccentric, Critchlow, and Cyril, the son, grown from a wayward schoolboy to a selfish student of art, leaves Constance alone in her old home.

Book 3 takes up Sophia's experiences from her impulsive flight to London with Gerald Scales, a traveling salesman, to their marriage and their move to Paris. Gerald proves to be a profligate spendthrift who delights in shocking Sophia and negligently wounds her sensibilities in terrible ways. He deserts her. She falls ill and is rescued by Chirac, a former friend of Gerald, who falls in love with her. She acquires a boardinghouse, endures the siege of Paris and the difficulties of the Commune, makes money, and indirectly drives Chirac to his death.

Book 4 presents the discovery of Sophia by a friend of her nephew, Cyril. Constance persuades Sophia to take up residence once more in her old home. Dull routine overtakes both women, until a message comes for Sophia to visit her dying husband in Manchester. The shock and the trip together kill her. Constance outlives her for very few years, succumbing at last to complications of a chill taken while voting against modern trends in Bursley.

This is the surface narrative. Except for the switchback in time in book 3, the events are chronologically arranged. Seemingly there is nothing spectacular in story or form to attract the reader. Yet the experience of reading this narrative is absorbing. At first the reader is fascinated by the insight and the accuracy with which Bennett catches all the moods of his various personalities and the extent to which he makes the reader care about these people. As the reader pays closer attention to Bennett's technique, he realizes that not one detail is included merely for effect; that not one detail stands alone in the text; not one minor character is mentioned, only to disappear; each recurs, or is built upon, to produce that sense of enduring community in which the major figures have their being.

The opening sentence names the two major figures and through an ironic contradiction begins to indicate their oblivion to what the world would consider is the narrowness of their existence. But the perception of the narrowness of one's world is relative to the level of cultivation of one's mind. The world of a child, who is not actually abused, is the world of its wonder, no matter where it is. How long the wonder lasts depends upon the circumstances. The world of the Baines girls has provided them with scope for wonder well into their teens. Thus, the paragraph that follows the opening sentence humorously sets the girls on the fifty-third parallel of latitude and proceeds to give a geological survey of the area beyond their county, emphasizing the desire, which is apparent in each district, to guard jealously local distinctions.

For several paragraphs Bennett banteringly draws the survey ever closer to the exact position of the two girls, while giving a sociological outline. Eventually the Baines shop is in focus, its exterior a mute testimony to Mr. Baines's business principles, predominant among which is his great objection to "puffing," that is, self-advertisement. And in the showroom window we see the girls with their noses pressed against the glass.

Bennett shapes the warmly humorous attitude that is appropriate to the naive, coltish, charming girls at this stage. His use of the usual "Roman nose," as an attribute of beauty, his inclusion of "quivering" sensibilities, is combined surprisingly with his reference to the "circulation of the blood." This juxtaposition brings to the reader's attention the perfect order only temporarily maintained in the human body in youth. The gradual disruption of this order into decay and death forms one of the themes poignantly presented in the novel. Ironically, we recognize that the girls have everything to learn and we expect to follow their learning process. But no sad note sounds in this paragraph; all is light and amusing.

Within the space of eight paragraphs Bennett delineates the county, the district, the town. He gives the significant features of St. Luke's Square which frames the girls' lives, mentioning particularly Critchlow's chemist shop; the significant features of their home, mentioning the inconvenience of its structure; the significant attitude of their father, which reaches beyond his grave; and the mood of the girls, which is subject to mercurial change. The Wakes Week "when the shocking always happened"[6] (4) is mentioned, and the problem of signboards and clearance sales. All of these details are essential in the narrative. The daily events, even the very shape of St. Luke's Square, are vital elements in producing the various crises in the novel.

But for the retail trade of the Square Gerald Scales would never have come to be noticed by Sophia Baines. But for the steepness of its slope, which invited the daring, eleven-year-old Dick Povey to test the speed of his "boneshaker" in the Square and fall at the Baines's door, Samuel Povey, Constance's huband, would never have ventured to make the acquaintance of his more illustrious cousin, Daniel, and become involved in his trial for murder. But for Critchlow's obstinate attentions, old John Baines might have succumbed to his inertia years before and not have required Sophia's vigilance on the day he died. But for the shocking death of an elephant in the Wakes Week celebrations, Sophia might not have been left alone to look after her father, nor Scales have stayed in the district to meet her, and John Baines would not have died from her negligence. But for Critchlow's cruel comments after the death, Sophia might not have given up her ambition to teach and fallen under Scales's sway.

The reader can select even a minor figure, or any apparently insignificant event, and discover that Bennett develops relationships from each of them which are significantly interwoven throughout the narrative. For instance, that which fascinates the young girls as they press their noses against the showroom window is a view of Maggie, their middle-aged servant, heading up the Square to a rendezvous with her twelfth boyfriend. This event serves to highlight the attitude of the young girls to the nature of love. Naively, they are incredulous that any but the beautiful and young could attract lovers; they feel that manifestations of passion in older people are grotesque.

In introducing Maggie, Bennett sketches the life the drudge has lived in the cellars of the Baines house. He lays bare the hardships that Maggie accepts and her employers ignore. At intervals, Maggie's progress through life is documented, complementing the passing of the girls' lives. She leaves the Baines's employment, marries a drunkard, has several children; they grow up and disappear from the narrative. These events are merely mentioned, yet the reader through them is made constantly aware of the relentless passage of time. At the same time, the reader follows these girls' experiences in love. For Sophia this involves dealing with aged French courtesans and old roués. Her own love affair has made it impossible for her to view these aging lovers with anything but the disgust she had felt in her youth for the hopeful Maggie. Understandings flow from Bennett's treatment of these details as illuminating connections are recognized.

Two critics of Bennett's novel have stated that in his treatment of Maggie and of her domain Bennett begins to use two other important literary devices in making his meanings clear—what E. K. Brown calls "rhythm,"[7] and what James Hepburn recognizes as symbolism.[8] In Mr. Brown's assessment of the repetition of Sophia's life of experiences of aged lovers she appears incapable of changing her girlhood notion that they are all old fools. Incapacity to change sufficiently mars Sophia's progress in life.

In Mr. Hepburn's examination of Bennett's techniques he finds Maggie's cave one of the more important symbols linking with other images and metaphors to stress secret feelings. As this study shows, Sophia's experiences shock her into repressions where her secret feelings become so deeply buried that, indeed, she almost ceases to feel. Although Mr. Hepburn does not state the fact, it is implicit in his treatment of the symbolism, that Bennett uses these patternings to support the larger ironies of his tale.

The combination of circumstances with their inevitable results is impressively shaped by Bennett to proceed with a relentlessness that becomes at times fearful. Set at appropriate intervals in the steady flow of everyday affairs are events that shock the reader out of any complacency, as they shock the characters who experience them out of the ruts they have occupied comfortably.

There is the matter of Mr. Povey's tooth. To trace Bennett's subtle treatment of the gradual destruction of innocence and optimism in the beautiful, intelligent Sophia would require an exegesis far too long for the discussion here. However, as brief an account as possible of the crisis that occurs in the relationship of the two sisters, and that revolves around the tooth, will give some idea of Bennett's method throughout the narrative.

After the girls turn from watching Maggie go up the Square, Sophia joyfully suggests some entertainment. The more staid Constance wishes to do needlework for her mother's birthday. Her tone in refusing Sophia's suggestion makes the younger sister annoyed that Constance has begun to take on grown-up airs. Her irrepressible spirits lead her from one act of bravado to another.

First, she dares to parade in her mother's new skirt, astonishing her quiet sister; then, when Mr. Povey requires attention for his toothache, she puts sewing pliers in Mr. Povey's mouth and plucks out one dangling tooth as he sleeps from an excess of laudanum the girls had given him. Mr. Povey jumps awake, but Sophia, with hand behind her back, has the tooth. A fish hawker's cry enables Sophia to insist that they buy mussels for supper in order that she may get outside the door to laugh. Later, while eating mussels, Mr. Povey suddenly discovers the missing tooth. He is convinced he swallowed it. Sophia loses all control and rushes from the parlor to indulge in hysterical laughter in the cutting-room of the shop.

There she stays for such a long time that she feels uneasy at not being sought out. She wonders why Constance stays with Mr. Povey in the drawing room. Forlorn, she cannot bring herself to join them, but wanders around the house, finally going to her room. She expects Constance to come. As Mr. Critchlow leaves after his visit to her father, as Maggie returns to her duties in the kitchen, as Mr. Povey retires for the night, as her mother returns from her errands, as night falls, Sophia waits and dozes. She is awakened by her mother's knock upon Mr. Povey's door. She watches her mother and Constance leave Mr. Povey's door and enter her father's room. Jealously, Sophia recognizes that her older sister has more of her parents' confidence than she does.

Finally, when Constance comes to their bedroom, Sophia is ready to be irritable. She provokes Constance with ironic comments upon Mr. Povey's condition and shocks her with the fact that she possesses the tooth. But she laughs so long that her own annoyance leaves her. However, Constance has been stirred to righteous anger. She demands that the tooth be given her to throw away. Sophia, her gaiety gone, refuses. They stare at each other savagely. Then Constance walks away to brush her hair. After a moment Sophia slips out of bed to place the tooth in her sewing-box. Constance, five minutes later, says her prayers and, having said them, walks straight to Sophia's sewing-box, takes the tooth and flings it out the window. Bennett writes:

"There!" she exclaimed nervously.
She had accomplished this inconceivable transgression of the code of honour, beyond all undoing, before Sophia could recover from the

stupefaction of seeing her sacred work-box impudently violated. In a single moment one of Sophia's chief ideals had been smashed utterly, and that by the sweetest, gentlest creature she had ever known. It was a revealing experience for Sophia—and also for Constance. And it frightened them equally. . . . Within minutes Constance is in bed, silence reigns for a while, then:

"And if you want to know," said Constance in a tone that mingled amicableness with righteousness, "mother's decided with Aunt Harriet that we are *both* to leave school next term." (31-32)

Bennett's insight into the minds of youth, his grasp of the psychology of these girls, his accuracy in revealing his knowledge by delineating all the aspects that caused this particular crisis, his inclusion of the anticlimactic detail which naturally rounds out this episode, but is also the basis for the next coil of action spiraling to an explosion, prove his mastery of his craft. Not one of the series of actions given in synopsis above is extraneous to this crisis, not one but has ramifications throughout the remainder of the novel. Sophia's precipitate actions characterize her until her spirit has been crushed in Paris. Constance's need to be motherly to Mr. Povey is the first sign that her general benevolence is taking a special turn in his case. Her unusual fierceness and desperate act to protect his dignity mark the degree of her attachment. The slightly younger Sophia, heart-free, is shaken when ethics are discarded in emotional tumult. Constance, no less surprised, rallies herself with the sharing of some news. She cannot know that any reference to confidences with her mother would exacerbate Sophia's feelings in this crisis. The reader cannot know if Sophia's reaction to leaving school would be the same whether this incident had occurred or not. All the reader can be sure of is that hearing of it first at this particular time Sophia's sense of being pushed, of being defeated, would force her to rebel.

Her rebellion is the substance of the next long chapter and it ends with Mrs. Baines's defeat. So far, the substance of three chapters, comprising three days in the lives of the main characters, has been indicated. But between chapter 3 and the opening of chapter 4 two years have passed. The nature of the first three chapters, the seemingly leisurely pace, the mass of details, actually mask Bennett's careful selection of events to highlight. He chooses to omit years and happenings in such a way that the reader feels nothing has been omitted or missed. A sense of the long years through which these girls change into tired old women is fully felt. Yet that sense does not produce an impression of a dull or dragging text. Each chapter with its numbered sections carefully documents varying crises so that the reader moves from one emotional tumult to the next, apparently without pause.

The ease with which Bennett expands hours in paragraphs or condenses months in a sentence makes the reader accept his handling of time as if it were the natural passage of clock-time, while he preserves simultaneously for the reader his awareness that a minute may seem an hour, or an hour a fleeting second. His concluding paragraph for book 1, describing Mrs. Baines retiring to Axe, catches simply and poignantly the end of one cycle while indicating its place in the endless cycle of human existence.

The course of Constance's married life is carried to the point where she has reached the age her mother had reached when she went to Axe. She too is a widow and she too has suffered the trials of rearing a wayward child. The cry of her soul as book 2 ends echoes her mother's. Yet the experience of reading book 2 is not a repetitive one. Constance's nature is quite different from her mother's, her relationship with her child is different again, and the crises in her life develop in different areas. The difference is as much the result of the gradual changes in the tenor of society after a generation has passed as the result of a different combination of personalities reacting upon each other, the reader recognizes.

Bennett succeeds in suggesting her child's infancy and childhood with highly detailed presentations of very few incidents. The baby's-eye-view of rolling on the carpet before a fire is effectively done; his fifth-year birthday party provides a striking display of Bennett's knowledge of the child's world; the crisis of his thievery as a schoolboy, his behavior with Amy, the Povey's servant; all these instances give the reader a remarkably vivid sense of the emotional crests and troughs in the ordinary lives of the Povey family.

Then comes the horror of Daniel Povey's murder of his wife. It comes to be the climax of the diffident Samuel's life. The growth of his faith that Daniel cannot be hung for murder is powerfully delineated and it becomes one with his belief in himself. After Daniel is hanged, Samuel succumbs to pneumonia. The remaining three chapters of book 2 sketch the gradual reduction of the widow's activities. Her thoughts of Sophia, recurring throughout book 2 and at its end, make a simple link with book 3.

In book 3 Bennett follows nineteen-year-old Sophia in her nervous flight to London and Gerald Scales. Her fiercely held ideals have not prevented her from stealing ten pounds from her Aunt Harriet, but they do prevent her from perceiving that Gerald Scales is a dishonorable wretch. Bennett again gives very few events to dramatize Sophia's brutal initiation to the life Gerald would have her lead in Paris. His behavior in a fashionable restaurant causes her to be left alone, the object of pity and scorn in a room full of cocottes. Her exposure at Auxerre to the horrors of a public execution by guillotine, with all the attendant madness of the French rabble, removes the shreds of her respect for him. These episodes are drawn by Bennett with great economy, yet with vividly authentic strokes. The long weeks of Sophia's illness, the years of her struggle to survive in France as the Napoleonic empire collapsed, her gradual change into the cold, capable boarding mistress, are carefully delineated.

Obviously, there is a symmetry in the shaping of the blocks of this narrative, a symmetry not in outline only, but in the massing and patterning of all the details. This proportion gives no sense of being arbitrarily imposed; it is organic. The ironies of the form given to the events of the narrative cannot be isolated for consideration from the cumulative effects of powerful individual scenes and descriptive passages carefully wrought by Bennett at intervals throughout the novel. These are not set pieces which stand out from the flow of the narrative, but they are scenes with informing links of their own which spring to the mind of the reader after he has completed reading the novel. One of the first is that in which Sophia is sent to sit with her invalid father in the midst of the crisis concerning her wish not to leave school. With his hot dry hand clutching her arm, he tells her he cannot allow her to teach. Bennett accurately captures her sense of the enormity of this injustice through the contrast of her vital capacity with her father's impotent fragility. This old man, neglected by Sophia during another vigil, dies of asphyxia after slipping partway out of bed. Bennett writes of Critchlow and the widow:

They knew not that they were gazing at a vanished era. . . . Mid-Victorian England lay on that mahogany bed. Ideals had passed away with John Baines. It is thus that ideals die; not in the conventional pageantry of honoured death, but sorrily, ignobly, while one's head is turned. (76)

Such is Sophia's horror at her neglect that she gives up her hard-won ambition and enters the shop. But when Gerald Scales no longer comes as salesman for Birkenshaw's, Sophia faces the fact that she had given up teaching less for her part in her father's death than for her knowledge that Gerald frequented her father's shop. She is shamed in her self-deception. When the tumultuous spirit of Sophia carries her with Gerald to Paris and thence to Auxerre, Bennett writes:

And Sophia waited, horror-struck. . . . Why was she in this strange, incomprehensible town, foreign and inimical to her, watching with agonized glance this cruel, obscene spectacle? Her sensibilities were all a bleeding mass of wounds. (320)

Sophia, despising Gerald from the day of the execution, is abandoned by him but rescued by Chirac. Following her compassionate but firm repulse of his love, he appears to be dying of a broken heart. Sophia despises his weakness, but smelling smoke one night, she finds Chirac asleep near a lighted cooking lamp. Bennett writes:

Chirac made a heart-rending spectacle, and Sophia was aware of deep and painful emotion in seeing him thus. . . . His attitude had the unconsidered and violent prostration of an overspent dog. . . . It recalled Sophia to a sense of the inner mysteries of life, reminding her somehow that humanity walks ever on a thin crust over terrific abysses. She did not physically shudder; but her soul shuddered. (409)

Finally, Sophia is called to the house where Gerald Scales, over seventy, lies in death. She had not seen him for more than thirty years. Alone, she gazes at him.

She was not sorry that Gerald had wasted his life, nor that he was a shame
to his years and to her. The manner of his life was of no importance. What
affected her was that he had once been young, and that he had grown old,
and was now dead. . . . "Yet a little while", she thought, "and I shall be
lying on a bed like that! And what shall I have lived for? What is the
meaning of it?" The riddle of life itself was killing her, and she seemed to
drown in a sea of inexpressible sorrow. (540)

These excerpts, although describing emotional crises at widely
separated stages in Sophia's life, have a consistency in somberness
of tone that marks Sophia as Bennett's tragic heroine in the novel.
Her temperament and her circumstances prove to be a destructive
combination. Her disillusionment with life began early; for her, no
ideal has proved lasting. The riddle of her life does indeed kill her.
The ideals of mid-Victorian England which had passed away with
her father were replaced by deadening materialistic aims for the
greater part of her life; all ideals are not thereby to be discredited.
Those ideals that are not merely period mores, that embody some
of the permanent longings of the human soul, those remain to be
fought for. But in repression Sophia lost all her ideals, lost the
source of her vitality, and died.

Sophia does not stand as the only heroine in the novel.
Constance, her name signifying the most notable aspect of her
nature, though the eldest, outlives her sister. She is the enduring
one, the one who tries to control her emotional upheavals with
commonsense. Her life does not include the horrors Sophia
endured. Bennett does not shape lengthy descriptive passages for
her. She is not given to pondering issues, but acts. The reader
remembers her carefully lettering price-tickets for the man she
marries, feeding their child in contentment, weeping as her
husband punishes their wayward boy, superintending her husband's dressing for the cold journey to the assizes, removing the
few traces of her husband's existence after he dies, patiently
embroidering painting smocks for her artistic son, determined not
to let Sophia domineer over her, proudly showing albums to young
neighbors.

The tenor of her life is even and restricted. Her view never
expands beyond the Square. As she lies dying, although she does
not know her attack is serious, Constance reflects upon the course
of Sophia's life and of her own. She pities Sophia

as a woman whose life had been wasted. . . . She did not consider that Fate had treated her very badly. . . . she had tasted triumphant hours. . . . When she surveyed her life, and life in general, she would think, with a sort of tart but not sour cheerfulness: "*Well, that is what life is!*" (575)

In Bennett's construction, neither Sophia's despairing question nor Constance's self-satisfied answer provide the conclusion of the novel. Both the penultimate and the final paragraphs are filled with ironies which must be considered. But before these paragraphs can be evaluated, the humorous cast of the entire novel needs review. Although the quotations from the novel and the discussion of its content presented here have certainly emphasized the somber, the pathetic, the tragic, there can be no doubt that the reader of the novel is very much aware of the comic in it. The opening presents a humorous setting of scene. Throughout the novel comic descriptions, comic episodes, comic characters modify the reader's impression of the total content.

The more lighthearted comic constructions permeate the first two books—the books of exuberant youth and successful married life. Ironic constructions permeate the two remaining books—the books of disillusionment, decay, and death. Bennett in book 1 humorously describes the poster of fashions that spurs Sophia to her first exhibition of high spirits; he lingers over the comic depiction of Sam Povey's behavior under the torture of toothache; he includes humorous touches in his description of the Baines kitchen. There is a warm delight in his presentation of Constance and Samuel "making history," as well as making love, with their production of tickets. There is the social comedy of his presentation of the Wesleyan Chapel congregation on New Year's Eve with the "pew-full" of distracted Baineses. He humorously treats Mrs. Baines's suspicions of Sophia's infatuation and Sophia's visions in linking mock-heroic imagery. The comedy of Povey's request for Constance's hand is cleverly done. The new dog's instant conquest of old Mrs. Baines, the joy of the expectant Povey parents, Povey's embarrassment when Constance uninhibitedly feeds her child before Miss Insull, Cyril's disgrace at his birthday party, all these incidents are filled with humor. And these incidents shape the reader's reactions to the seriously treated events in the characters' lives.

It is because so much humor complements the narrative of

Constance's life to middle age that the reader can accept her estimate of her own life as she lies dying. What Bennett achieves by his mixture is indicated in his effective comments on Samuel Povey's death:

A casual death, scarce noticed in the reaction after the great febrile demonstration! Besides, Samuel Povey never could impose himself on the burgesses. He lacked individuality. He was little. I have often laughed at Samuel Povey. But I liked and respected him. He was a very honest man. I have always been glad to think that, at the end of his life, destiny took hold of him and displayed, to the observant, the vein of greatness which runs through every soul without exception. He embraced a cause, lost it, and died of it. (238-239)

Through the eyes of the Comic Spirit Samuel is viewed and he does impose himself on the reader. His characterization, through comedy, is sufficiently realized in the novel.

But with the sad events of Sophia's life the humor becomes ironic. Its presence is found less in small illustrative incidents than in the shaping of the larger movements of the last two Books. The irony of Sophia's headlong pursuit of romance in spite of the warnings of her commonsense in the earlier part of her career and her ruthless pursuit of commonsense to the destruction of romance in the later part of her career is made clear. Gerald Scales's parallel desertions of her, first in a London hotel and then in a Paris hotel, are shaped in irony. There is the irony of Sophia's refusal to return to Bursley while attempting to impose Bursley standards and way of life within the most notorious street in Paris. When the sisters join forces in Bursley, ironically the strong-willed Sophia is forced to capitulate to the mass of Constance's inertia. Finally, and again ironically, all the material possessions so hoarded by Constance and the money so hardly won by Sophia will be inconsequentially dispersed by their one descendant.

The reader comes then to estimate the effect of the two paragraphs that conclude the narrative. The penultimate paragraph, after mentioning Cyril's absence from his mother's funeral and his inheritance of all the wealth, brings Charles Critchlow, chemist, forward for the last time. He is the Methuselah of the Square. He has attended with sardonic glee every calamity of the Baines family. His comments, cruel but always a realist's estimate, have provided reacting-points for the characters and for the reader throughout the text. He is more than a Dickensian-type caricature of Shakespeare's bitter-tongued Jaques. His pronouncement at Constance's funeral that "It's a pity her didn't live long enough to hear as Federation is going on after all! That would ha' worritted her!" (477) is not simply a callous dismissal of a heroine in the novel, but a clear-eyed realist's conclusion of the ridiculousness of an old woman's attempt to prevent change in a world whose basis is change.

With the effects of this paragraph the reader must join that of the final paragraph. Only the servant and Sophia's ancient, offensive French poodle are left in the house as the funeral procession of Constance sets out. The tearful servant places dinner for the dog who, conscious of her deranged day, first walks away from it, but, after some minutes, goes to it again. Is one to assume that, in Eliot's phrase, Bennett ends his tale of generations "not with a bang but a whimper"? Certainly, the objective reader tutored by Critchlow might assume so. As the tale is shaped, however, it is not the sad story of Sophia that concludes the narrative, but the more satisfying story of Constance. To the title of book 2—"What Life Is," Bennett adds Constance's reflection on her own—"That is what life is." His humorous presentations and his ironic shapings make the reader aware that life does not have to be what his people in *The Old Wives' Tale* make of theirs. But, in fact, given their backgrounds, their temperaments, their sets of illusions, their choices, it could not indeed be otherwise for them. He has demonstrated the pattern, his incidents all have "fitness," and the reader gains a "moral wisdom by the tracing everywhere of cause and effect." The irreconcilables and absurdities in the lives of his figures have been delineated. From the ridiculous isolationism humorously depicted in the opening description of the larger environment to the careful presentation of the absurd egotism of the pampered dog viewed in the empty house at the end, Bennett draws from his reader the sympathetic smile at human foibles. His *Old Wives' Tale* is then an "unassailable"[9] human comedy.

Chapter Five
The Apex of Bennett's Career

At the height of his creative power, Bennett in 1909 produced an unusual novel called *The Glimpse*, then, in 1910, turned his most searching gaze upon the painful period of his youth, the period in midlife of his courtship, and the early years of his marriage. Riding a wave of emotional release in the establishment of a new home with an exotic, talented wife, and with the acclaim of his recent successes in *Buried Alive* and *The Old Wives' Tale* supporting him, he found the courage to examine his past and the wisdom to assess his present with an honesty that is startling and refreshing. His unerring accuracy in locating the forms, the courses, and the effects of strains in relationships link him with earlier writers like George Eliot and Anthony Trollope, with contemporaries like Henry James, and helped pave the way for the fine discriminations found in younger writers like D. H. Lawrence and Virginia Woolf.[1]

The most important result of his confident efforts is the trilogy: *Clayhanger* (1910), *Hilda Lessways* (1911), and *These Twain* (1916). A fourth novel, *The Roll Call* (1918), features Hilda Lessway's son George Cannon, but it was not written to be included or considered with the other three. Following the first two novels of the Clayhanger series, Bennett wrote *The Card* (1911), *The Regent* (1913), and *The Price of Love* (1914) before completing the trilogy with *These Twain* (1915). Within the trilogy readers find considerable variation in value. General assessment places the first high in achievement, the second a decided falling away, the third a partial recovery. This study verifies the general valuations of the novels but modifies assessment of the second and third books.

The Glimpse

Before looking more closely at his experiences of life in the Potteries, Bennett was attracted to a subject very different from his usual choices. On May 23, 1908, he had finished a short story entitled "The Glimpse" for *Black and White* which he felt was "too good, too spiritual,"[2] It was refused by that magazine, offered to Ford Madox Ford for the *English Reivew*, and ultimately published in the *New Age*, November 4, 1909.[3] In November, 1908 he had read H. G. Wells's *First and Last Things*. Writing about the book, he questioned Wells's summary negative treatment of immortality and the transmigration of souls, and stated that he was a believer in the transmigration of souls as "the theory which presents fewest difficulties."[4] Wells's book renewed Bennett's interest in the subject and he expanded earlier material into the novel *The Glimpse* (1909), subtitled *An Adventure of the Soul.*

It is a tour de force, a variation of the notion that a man at the point of death relives his entire life in seconds. Here Bennett's central figure experiences in a few hours of death the life of the human race and, beyond that, relives the life of the planet and the cosmos. It is a strange exploration of temperament reminiscent at times of the excesses found in *Sacred and Profane Love*. Like the earlier novel, *The Glimpse* features a first-person narrator, Maurice Loring. Unlike the highly emotional Carlotta, Loring presents himself as an intellectual valuing reason and decorum above all virtues. He is a successful music critic, an art historian with highly cultivated aesthetic tastes, and the husband of a beautiful woman.

His narrative is divided into three books. The first traces his development as a critic, his marriage to Inez, the deterioration of their relationship culminating in an angry confrontation provoking Loring's collapse and apparent death. Book 2 traces the experiences of Loring's spirit as it gradually moves from its association with earthly things, through widening and deepening levels of awareness to an abandonment of self, then passes through all the stages of the evolution of the universe to the very point of its origins, when an insistent sound seems to drown out all other awareness, and his soul is drawn inexorably back to his body. Book 3 opens as Loring regains consciousness, shocking his wife and servants who have proceeded with the funeral arrangements. Inez dies from a poison taken earlier in a frenzy of guilt and grief for Loring's supposed death. The remainder of the section shows Loring resolving all difficulties in his various relationships by relying on an attitude of mind acquired during the period of his "death." Loring realizes that a malaise of years had its source in his egoism, that happiness can only come to those who "spiritually coalesce"[5] with their fellows.

Because Loring is a vehicle for the indulgence of a fantasy, neither he nor the characters he tells us about approach the reality of Bennett's best characterizations. Milieu is negligible when compared to the significance of milieu in the Five Towns novels. However, the milieu of book 2 constitutes an ingenious feat of imagination. The plot shows Bennett's usual competence, but in the end it only serves to make the reader aware of the pose taken by the author. The novel is merely a clever exercise.

Bennett remarked in his journal that "the first and third part of 'The Glimpse' contained a lot of essentially autobiographical stuff."[6] It is possible to relate Loring's attitudes and the mutual incomprehension existing between him and his wife Inez in part 1 to a developing situation between Bennett and his wife. It is also possible to see the tolerance and efforts to understand, typical of Loring in part 3, as attributes Bennett felt he was struggling toward. Some of his journal entries for 1909 verify this continuing effort in Bennett's life. Meanwhile, throughout the period of the production of *The Glimpse* Bennett was researching background material for *Clayhanger* which he planned to begin in January, 1910. Although including much more autobiographical material, it is very different indeed from the arbitrariness of *The Glimpse*. Nevertheless, Loring's discovery of an important attitude of mind links him with Clayhanger who is far more subtly treated in his battle against egoism.

Clayhanger

One modern critic recognizing the success of *Clayhanger* calls it "a stunningly rich novel of provincial family life."[7] Its greatest strength is Bennett's remarkable realization of a sensitive portrait of the growth of a lovable young man. The chapters are grouped into Books and subdivided into sections. Edwin Clayhanger is introduced at the moving moment of school-leaving. He gazes over a canal bridge and reflects upon his future. Bennett uses the moment to highlight aspects of the scene which "have everything to do"[8] with Edwin and "with the history of each of the two hundred thousand souls in the Five Towns" (3-4). Edwin is described as having an "extraordinarily wistful look of innocence and simplicity . . ." (4). This is followed by the comment:

It seemed rather a shame, it seemed even tragic, that this naive, simple creature, with his straightforward and friendly eyes so eager to believe in appearances, . . . must soon be transformed into a man, wary, incredulous, detracting." (4)

However, Edwin's view of himself is that of "a hardened sort of brute, free of illusions" (5). The poles of the exterior and interior views are maintained with variations throughout the trilogy.

Chapter 2 continues to stress the demarcation point in Edwin's life which is to initiate the establishment of who Edwin is. The omniscient narrator says: "He knew, however, nothing of natural history, and in particular of himself, of the mechanism of the body and mind, through which his soul had to express and fulfil itself" (11). The novel presents the process by which Edwin achieves his unique realization. The narrator ironically stresses the extent of the ignorance from which Edwin must start and catches, in a simile ending the following paragraph, the Alice-through-the-looking-glass-world that is characterized by the conglomeration of unrelated facts the boy has absorbed from school. Bennett describes Edwin's uneasiness that his education did not fit him to arrive at answers; his desire, "and there was real passion in his desire—to do his best, to exhaust himself in doing his best, in living according to his conscience" (15).

This attitude surfacing in the young graduate is made his distinguishing characteristic carefully drawn in the selected events of the novel. The course taken presents the extension and refinement of this attitude in Edwin. Obviously, the emphasis of the novel moves it from the plane of *The Old Wives' Tale*, where Bennett brilliantly documents primarily the exterior of his heroines and their situations in capturing their sense of life, to the plane where he equally brilliantly traces primarily the mental states and growth of awareness produced in the hero in response to external events. Sophia and Constance are much less self-conscious than Edwin.

The narrative carries Edwin from school to servitude in his father's print shop. His father Darius considers Edwin a pampered child when judged by his own childhood. Darius secretly never forgets his having been in the workhouse when a boy, his rescue by his old Sunday School teacher Shushions, his slavery in the pot-banks from the age of seven, and the miracle of his progression to be a successful printer. He considers his printshop an inestimable prize for Edwin.

In book 2 Edwin's interest in architecture leads to friendship with the affluent Orgreave family in whose home he meets Hilda Lessways, the love of his life. When Edwin requests an increase in salary in order to plan for his marriage, his father's obtuseness and tyranny drive Edwin to thoughts of future power and revenge when his father has grown old. His hopes of Hilda, his disgust with his father, merge into a blank despair when he receives the astonishing news that she was speedily married in Brighton.

Book 3 presents Darius's shock upon learning that his savior Shushions is dying in a workhouse, and his frantic efforts to arrange an appropriate funeral for the old man. Strong symptoms of a debilitating disease appear in Darius from the day of the funeral. The remainder of this section traces his two-year decline to death before his appalled son. In book 4 Edwin, enjoying total authority in his home and in his work, reviews what he is making of his life. He meets Hilda's son George at the Orgreaves and, after a decade, pursues again his old interest in George's mother and accepts a new commitment to marry her.

This synopsis of events indicates clearly the shift in emphasis of this novel from that of its acclaimed forerunner. Here a whole lifetime is not portrayed, although the experience of generations is captured. The reader follows only two decades in the hero's life and the pivotal events are few. However, Bennett's strength in documenting the pressure of daily occurrences as the significant context for the main events, and his power of suggesting the rolling on of years in the area, are so synthesized that it is more difficult than with *The Old Wives' Tale* to illustrate what is, in accumulation, the abiding value of the novel.

The clash between generations and between personality types and the asserting of individuality are made central concerns in *Clayhanger*. The mutual incomprehension of Darius and Edwin overwhelming their urge to love each other is authentically given the proportions of tragedy. The first encounter of Edwin and his father occurs in book 1, chapter 3, when Edwin arriving from school meets his father with the ancient Shushions on the shop steps. Neither the reader nor Edwin knows why Darius unusually shows emotion, nor why, at sight of Edwin, Shushions sheds a tear. Edwin's usual quiet self-possession before the loud dictatorship of his father is modified to a puzzled humility before the spectacle of the tear.

In chapters 4 and 5, Bennett movingly reveals the "fearful secret" of Darius's infancy which has produced the belligerent independence of the grown man along with his reverence of Shushions and his view of his son's future. Edwin, not knowing his father's past, cannot appreciate the wellsprings of his behavior nor properly estimate his father's aims. Edwin never gains this insight. The reader, having it, finds the succession of father-son encounters made more poignant. All Darius's efforts are, he believes, entirely for his son and daughters, whereas Edwin can only see these efforts as the selfish moves of a tyrannical egoist.

Bennett constructs illustrative scenes like the one in chapter 11. Edwin, having claimed an attic room adjoining his own as a sign of his new status of salaried employee, sits there in a solitude the family usually respects, but is surprised by his father. Previously, Edwin had carried out a small transaction in his father's absence at Manchester. There is some dialogue reminiscent of the equally rare moment of communication between Anna and her father. Here Darius's mood is so modified by Edwin's having done the business successfully and by his own bargain purchase of machinery in Manchester, that he does not abruptly order Edwin off to bed, but leans over Edwin's chair to see his drawings. Edwin seizes the moment to state clearly that he wants to be an architect.

Anna's father had had a wry understanding of the beginning of romance in his daughter. Darius scarcely notices his son's declaration, while Edwin believes it had been registered and acknowledged. Edwin had many times tried to voice his ambition to members of his family, but failed. His bold statement to his father appears momentous to him. He cannot conceive that his words are negligible to his father. The roots of future disagreements are clearly set here in a moment of warmth which itself will exacerbate by disappointed expectations the anger in clashes to come.

In building the tensions between father and son, Bennett presents Darius mainly from an exterior view while Edwin's consciousness is registered. Darius is not thereby removed from the reader's sympathy; his powerful mass is seen to move with the relentlessness of the ponderous machines he has gathered around him; yet his inarticulateness is sometimes interpreted and voiced by members of the family like Auntie Hamps who entirely admires him. The reader recognizes the severe limitations of the old man, but understands fully his achievements and aims. Edwin's great sense of grievance against his father is equally established. The pathos of the situation is made acutely moving in that there is no clear villain and victim; neither is right and the other wrong. They are both right in their understandings of circumstances, yet inevitably at cross-purposes. Bennett, in the three books that include Darius, shapes the movement in mounting waves of frustration and anger for Edwin which only end when Darius is laid aside to die. Following the curves of Edwin's experience, Darius's succession of assumptions, expectations, disappointments, satisfactions, provide the reader with a complex dual view.

His father's collapse after Shushion's funeral surprises Edwin out of the imprisoning routine. The contradictions in his responses to his father's dismaying deterioration are particularized without sentimentality. The painful incidents of Enoch Bennett's death are here recaptured with an honesty that remarkably illuminates the actual experience and the fictional one. As Edwin gains a control over his father more complete than ever he had longed for in his vengeful moments, he finds his power not satisfying, but terrible. Edwin discovers in his father's safe a carefully saved drawing he had made as a child, evidence of his father's pride in him, and he finds his father's business acumen many times documented. His readjustment of his assessment of his father enables him to control his irritations, to recognize an affection, and to be gentle with the old man at the end.

With Darius's death an impressive personality is removed from the novel, a significant conflict ended. Some readers feel that life leaves the novel at this point. But there is all of book 4 to follow. Bennett's achievements in the last book depend upon the impressions made in book 2. There, Edwin meets and commits himself to Hilda Lessways, the only other dominant personality in his life. In book 4, after a ten-year gap, this relationship is renewed and brought to the marriage avowal.

Within books 2 and 4 tensions develop between Hilda and Edwin that parallel the tensions between Darius and Edwin. Hilda appears as enigmatic to Edwin as his father. But where the father's mystery and seeming cruelty to his son overwhelms the love the boy might have felt for him, the girl's mystery and seeming cruelty to the young man do not destroy the love he feels for her. Bennett adequately develops the major sources of the spell she casts in these books.

Edwin has absorbed little knowledge of women up to his twenty-third year. In pursuing privacy for himself and granting privacy to his sisters and father throughout his youth, Edwin has practically isolated himself from the usual family concourse. Consequently, he seldom observes the expressions, tones, etc., of the girls, and frequently being surprised by their behavior, he forms the notion that women are capricious and incalculable. The wry admiration he conceived for his Auntie Hamps extends by a little the narrow dimensions of his view. But it is not until he is disturbed by the attractions of the clog dancer and, later, remembers her when he is visited by the fashionable Janet Orgreave, that his sensations force him to revise the value of his association with women. Shortly afterward Edwin meets Hilda.

Bennett shapes few encounters for Edwin and Hilda in book 2; nevertheless, he devotes twelve of the twenty-one chapters to their relationship. At their first meeting Edwin, abashed by the elegant appointments of the Orgreave house, sees Hilda in surroundings that show her to be as isolated from it all as he is. Across the quiet conversation of the men rings the passionate voice of Hilda who contradicts what she heard. Edwin is startled, thrilled, and finds the sensation "dangerous," "threatening" (205). Later, uplifted by his first glass of wine, Edwin pronounces that there is no virtue in believing. In looking after the stir his statement made, Edwin catches Hilda's eyes "blazing on him" (211). Later, Hilda follows him to ask if he meant what he had said about believing. She shows, in her abrupt, demanding manner, that she is impressed; then, clasping his hand in farewell, she walks away leaving Edwin shaken by the physical contact. The elements of all successive encounters are here. The heightened emotions, the cryptic statements that astound, the shock of the simplest physical contact, the general attractions and repulsions, all document the powerful current drawing these two individuals together. After each encounter Edwin has the sense of being exhilaratingly alive.

Edwin's experience is set within a remarkably effective capturing

of the coils of a family life which includes the redoubtable Auntie
Hamps, Darius's sister-in-law; Maggie and Clara, his oldest and his
youngest daughters, respectively; Albert Benbow, later Clara's
husband and the father of her four children. Edwin's innate
reticence, his love of books, his gentleness, his diffidence, his
demand for logic, set him apart from them.

Each member of his family reacts to this difference in characteristic manner. His father hovers between awe and savage irritation;
stolid Maggie is all motherly acceptance; Clara, quick, pert,
jealous, takes his reticence for secretiveness and enjoys ferreting
out his intentions and embarrassing him; Auntie Hamps, the
splendidly dressed Chapel zealot, effulgently praises him, but
supports his father in all decisions. Albert, the vulgar opportunist,
juggles false camaraderie and reluctant deference. The multiple
gradations of these attitudes are rendered by a masterly selection
of detail and event given always the focus of Edwin's ingenuous
astonishment at human behavior, with his attendant efforts to
adjust his views and maintain equilibrium.

As this group experiences meals, work, visitings, jam-makings,
birthdays, holidays, illnesses, deaths, Bennett effectively distinguishes how, even for the most limited among them, the daily
round is fraught with emotional perils, exciting encounters, gulfs
of the unknown. With the manner and methods perfected in *The
Old Wives' Tale*, Bennett makes the reader appreciate the unique-
ness of a life, yet accept its ordinariness taken in the mass. The
mass itself has important presence in the novel. Bennett carefully
documents the experiences, the changes, overtaking whole populations, which give to individuals and to family groups the sense of
being pleasurably modern, yet fearful of the uncontrollable in the
tides of change.

Each aspect of the novel has its own interest; nevertheless, each
aspect serves in the end to illuminate Edwin. Instead of the sense
of overwhelming inevitableness which oppresses some readers of
The Old Wives' Tale, Bennett in *Clayhanger* induces the reader to
share Edwin's sense of the incalculable in himself, in his circle, and
in public events. His sense of surprise, his optimism of the
"romance of living," permeate the novel.

It is finally, then, in the definition of Edwin that Bennett shows
his greatest strength. Anna is brought only to the point of her
entry into adult life; Constance and Sophia are carried from birth

to death, but they are shallower figures. Edwin is given an expanded treatment from his sixteenth to his thirty-sixth year. He is made an intelligent, multifaceted man, whose predominant traits are extraordinarily attractive. He is viewed through an omniscient narration which primarily dramatizes Edwin's experiences from his perspective. The distance between reader and character is considerably narrower than the distance between the reader and Anna or the Baines girls. The feeling Bennett has for Edwin reminds one of the feeling Dickens had for David Copperfield, but Bennett does not fall into sentimentality.

In the beginning the reader sees the eager, friendly boy at school leaving with the qualification of the older generation's view that he must become a wary, incredulous, detracting man. The boy sees himself as already free of illusions. The plotted course shows both sets of assumptions to be wrong. The essence of Edwin's attractiveness in manhood is that in him is combined the straightforwardness, the eagerness, the capacity for wonder of a child, with the shrewdness, endurance, capability of a man of integrity. The process is not one of the destruction of values, but of the refinement and support of strengths with the reasonable control of weaknesses. The result is not the production of a saint, but the creation of a normally faulty human being one would welcome knowing.

Bennett shows the severely judging, logical side of Edwin's intellect being modified by the sympathetic, kind, ingenuous side of Edwin's emotions reaching a level of honesty in a balance of head and heart that is strongly appealing. In incident after incident Bennett exemplifies the spontaneous process, but the effect is not monotonous, for the reader shares with Edwin the sense of the mystery in experience. The elements of Edwin's response to Shushions are given full development in his relationship with his father following the clear onset of Darius's disease. Edwin tries to deal with his father's sorrow over Shushions's death. Bennett constructs a brief scene prefaced by a description of Edwin's attitude. Loathing sentimentality, knowing his father had not seen Shushions for years, he feels his father is indulging in the absurd sentimentality of a tyrant. He tries to be nonchalant and practical in the face of Darius's violent tears, thinking that he will have to treat the man "like a blooming child," but he is "startled and interested" (334).

In the choice of the word "interested" placed in this context, the reader himself is startled. It may first appear only to indicate how far from his father the son's sympathies lie. However, as Edwin's character develops, the reader recognizes the spectator in Edwin's conscious mind who appears most distinctly at moments of heightened emotion to add an extra dimension to the reactions being registered there. The effect could seem to be directed more to delineating the colder, intellectual side of Edwin, but, in fact, is directed toward the preservation in the man of the child's capacity to wonder. The chapter ends: "Devilish odd, all this! he reflected, as he got into bed. Assuredly he had disconcerting thoughts, not all unpleasant" (337). Bennett achieves the modifying callousness, but robs it of its sting by eliminating premeditation as in a child's sudden, cruel, but honest statement.

In experiencing the difficult death of his father Edwin gains stature. Bennett movingly, in great detail, captures the agony Edwin views. He feels disdain for those who can sleep while this mortal struggle goes on. In the evening the old man quietly dies. Edwin returns to his father's side feeling that there is something intolerably tragic in death: "But Edwin's distress was shot through and enlightened by his solemn satisfaction at the fact that destiny had allotted to him, Edwin, an experience of such profound and overwhelming grandeur" (449). The cast of Edwin's mind is constructive; his responses, never those of a facile optimist, are positive.

In Edwin's relationship with Hilda, Bennett captures the most delightful aspects of his character. His diffidence makes him constantly surprised when members of his circle show that they see more in him than even he can believe he has hidden within him. To Edwin, Hilda appears intelligent, independent, strong-minded, illogical, compassionate, demanding, surprising, physically exciting, like no other woman he has ever known. When his strong feeling for Hilda forces him to break through his own reserve at times, he experiences that vulnerability when the fear of misunderstanding is strong, the relief of communication is great, and the joy of being extended to one's best self is overwhelming. Bennett selects the incidents of the courtship to demonstrate all of these aspects in a progression that shows the growth of the untried youth from attraction to commitment, through disappointment, humiliation, to reaffirmation in a maturity that recognizes disparateness, but aims at unity through compromise.

The placement of the four books illuminates all that is necessary to appreciate fully Edwin's thoughts that conclude the novel: "The many problems and difficulties which marriage with her would raise seemed trivial in the light of her heart's magnificent and furious loyalty. He thought of the younger Edwin whom she had kissed into rapture, as of a boy too inexperienced in sorrow to appreciate this Hilda. He braced himself to the exquisite burden of life." His eager and apprehensive gaze, as he begins the voyage of discovery in marriage, gives *Clayhanger* an appropriate conclusion. The novel well deserves the praise that it is "perhaps the finest novel of its kind that any English writer has produced."[9]

Hilda Lessways

On the penultimate page of *Clayhanger* Hilda Lessways says to Edwin: "You'll never understand what I had to go through, and how I couldn't help myself . . . but I shall tell you . . . You *must* understand!" This statement is footnoted with the information that in the autumn of 1911 the author would publish a novel dealing with Hilda's history up to the day of her marriage with Edwin, and that a third novel dealing with the marriage would follow.

Hilda Lessways was published on schedule. At twenty-one Hilda is feeling a malaise that provokes her into arbitrary behavior toward her mother. Caroline Lessways, a simple, contented, nonaggressive widow, wants peace in her home. Although obviously family relationships are different, Bennett causes similar perceptions to arise in Edwin and Hilda. For example, Hilda thinks that with her intelligence if she cannot rule her mother amicably, then she is clumsy or wicked, or both.[10] Edwin in *Clayhanger* expresses a similar thought after a disagreement with Maggie (457). Bennett's obvious intention is to emphasize the unique combination of differences and similarities that powerfully draws these two together in marriage.

The events of Hilda's life, which must dovetail with her mysterious appearances in *Clayhanger*, are made to evolve out of inherent characteristics early apparent in Hilda as a child. Independent, precipitate action is typical of her. Willfully seeking a lawyer on her own to collect her mother's rents, she meets and is attracted by the handsome Cannon, who dispels her general malaise by suggesting she learn shorthand. A year later she is editorial secretary for a newspaper Cannon started, and when that fails, she accompanies his ailing sister to Brighton to run a boardinghouse. Cannon's success with the boardinghouse allows him to buy shares in a substantial hotel which enables him to propose marriage to Hilda. She recognizes her desire for him, but questions whether she loves him. Nevertheless, they marry only to have an angered servant reveal that the marriage is bigamous. Cannon leaves for America and Hilda decides to pursue her interest in Edwin. Meeting him at the Orgreaves and visiting his shop, she recognizes her love for him and realizes he loves her. Sarah's illness requires her to return to Brighton where, discovering she is pregnant, Hilda decides not to contact Edwin again. The novel ends with her reflections.

This plot reasonably accounts for the spaces in Hilda's life that do not appear in *Clayhanger*. It dictates considerable movement for Hilda so that for most of the novel she is set amid scenes foreign to her. The figures surrounding her are not drawn with the vivid portraiture of the figures surrounding Edwin. Hilda is projected by an omniscient narrator mainly functioning to describe her rather than to give the reader a sense of Hilda's consciousness. The consequences of the limitations reduce considerably the artistic merit of the novel. There is not that capturing of an essential milieu, of history, that sustains the major figures in *Clayhanger*. Something of his intention to capture "the point of view of the whole sex, against a mere background of masculinity" as expressed in Bennett's *Journal*,[11] may account for the more shadowed form of Cannon. Bennett does not expend on Hilda the passion of his presentation of Edwin. The loss in emotional intensity seriously detracts from the book. The reader is not convinced of Hilda's attraction to Cannon, nor of her disillusionment when it comes. Her integrity is damaged by a too-perfunctory treatment.

Nevertheless, *Hilda Lessways* is not negligible. Many facets of her personality necessarily omitted in the first novel are developed in the second to prepare one for the Hilda of *These Twain*. Hilda of *Hilda Lessways* mystifies Edwin, but, no longer mystifying the reader, interests the reader instead in her awkward, unsophisticated, unrecognized attempts to become the "New Woman."

Bennett throughout his life was fascinated by this phenomenon and reflects it in many of his novels. Here, he traces a striving in Hilda to be herself, to realize her potential while constantly trammelled by circumstances. That effort in her is to be compared to the same effort in Edwin. Bennett's demonstration of this fact enables him to conceive of the fundamental unity of the marriage of the battling couple in *These Twain*.

Consider that Hilda early acquires some of the prerogatives of a male in her household. She views her mother as an incapable woman and, having taken matters into her own hands, soon exults that she will be the first woman to work as a shorthand clerk in the area. Her sense of loss after her marriage to Cannon demonstrates this point. She thinks: "She was the wife. His existence went on mainly as before; hers was diverted, narrowed—fundamentally altered. Never now could she be enfranchised into the male world" (320).

That her perceptions across the years match Edwin's Bennett also demonstrates. When Hilda, viewing her mother's capable handling of Cannon's first visit, finds "her ideas concerning the business of domesticity were now mixed and opposing and irreconcileable, and she began to suspect that the basis of society might be more complex and confusing than in her youthful downrightness she had imagined" (43), we hear echoes of Edwin's recognitions (*Clayhanger*, 85, 89, 107). When she luxuriates in her brief freedom as mistress of the house and dictator to Florrie after her mother leaves for London, we hear echoes of Edwin's attitude toward his household after his father's death. When Hilda accepts the hospitality of the Orgreaves after meeting Janet in London, she secretly wonders what they see in her. Edwin expresses the same feeling in relation to the Orgreaves when he is first invited there. These parallels give the reader insights valuable in understanding *These Twain*. Before completing the trilogy, however, Bennett produced *The Card, The Regent*, and *The Price of Love*.

The Card, The Regent, and *The Price of Love*

In two months[12] Bennett produced *The Card*.[13] He described its form as having twelve chapters "each practically containing an episode or story complete in itself. It is purely humorous and light, but it is true to life. It describes the adventures of a Five Towns youth who rose from nothing to the highest dignities of the Five Towns, entirely by his knack of doing picturesque things."[14] Its episodic form worked well for serial publication. Its popular success led to its production in film, first in 1922, and again in 1952 when Alec Guiness starred as Denry.[15]

In creating Edward Henry (Denry) Machin, Bennett was expanding into novel size the adventures of a Five Towns type who had appeared in his short stories. Denry is given Bennett's own birth date and is shaped to be an exaggeration of traits Bennett knew were valued in his hometown, for which he shared a wry admiration, and which he knew some Londoners insisted upon seeing in himself. The portrait entertains on the level of slapstick comedy. Denry is ambitious to make fast, easy money, he is graceless, audacious, insensitive, but not vicious. He has the knack of seizing opportunities to promote himself out of what appear certain defeats. His optimism, his ingenuity, his proclivity for making headlines all provide much to laugh at. The only humanizing elements in his makeup are his relationship with his mother, a doughty seamstress who refuses to change her style of living to match Denry's increasing income, his surprising himself with his precipitate acts, his fears that he might have gone too far, and his relationship with Nellie, the young girl he marries.

All events give Bennett ample opportunity to include the dry, shrewd wit of the Five Towns in Denry's many sallies to all those he beats on his way to the top. The pugnacious Denry both attracts and repels. The novel is competently done for what is attempted in it, but its popularity surprised Bennett. He capitalized upon that success by writing its sequel *The Regent* in the same facetious tone.

The two novels Bennett published in 1913 and 1914 are also competent potboilers. *The Regent* (1913) is of lighter fare than *The Price of Love* (1914). Having thoroughly enjoyed writing *The Card*, experiencing all the excitements, disappointments, and difficulties of theatrical productions, he re-created Edward Henry Machin and set that incorrigible Five Towns character into the midst of the London theatrical dilemmas he was facing. In a letter to an American friend he said he was amusing himself with "a piece of facetiousness."[16] A sketch of the plot makes it obvious that Bennett was indulging in the relief of caricature. Significantly, in terms of the subject matter of the second novel of this period, and in terms of the more important study of *These Twain*, Denry sets out on his adventure in theater because the conditions of his marriage are disturbing him. The minor disorders in the home that cause him major irritation, his expectations and attitudes toward his wife, make Denry a comical mirror of aspects of Edwin Clayhanger that in turn Bennett wryly recognized in himself.

Denry, having bought an option on a theater in London, having on a dare taken a suite in an exclusive hotel, decides to live up to his income for awhile. He is visited by a former theatrical star, an actor-playwright, a manager, and a poet-playwright, who all assume that Denry is a rich fool from the country. He leads them on until he sees a way to use their own lack of integrity against them.

The targets for Bennett's caricature, beside the delusions of a former star, the guile of a manager, the arrogance of an incompetent poet, include affectations of the ruling classes, bullying of lawyers, the desire for publicity, the jealousies and gossiping of theatrical types, the confusion of first-night reviews. Denry succeeds against all odds to become sole proprietor of a theater built exactly to his specifications; he makes a questionable poetic drama into a one-hundred-performance success, with a faded, former star given renewed life as a leading lady who is forced for the first time to articulate so as to be understood in the galleries. He succeeds in toying with a theatrical siren, but avoids being caught, and returns to his wife and family in the Five Towns, having made all his adventures pay handsome dividends. The novel proves to be an entertaining romp with the provincial "doing the Londoners in the eye."

In contrast, *The Price of Love* does not remove its characters from the Five Towns, but gives less of the flavor of Five Towns types than one senses even in the eccentricities of Denry Machin. The cast of characters consists of Mrs. Malden; Rachel Fleckring, her young companion; Louis Fores and Julian Malden, her nephews; John Batchgrew, her solicitor; and Mrs. Toms, her housekeeper. Briefly stated, the events begin one evening, with Mrs. Malden and Rachel fearing thieves reported in the neighborhood, but taking comfort in that Julian will stay overnight. When Batchgrew brings over a thousand pounds from a recent property settlement, the women are made more nervous.

Louis attracts Rachel. She does not know he is embezzling funds from his employer, or that he finds part of his aunt's money upstairs and pockets it. By chance the money is burned as Mrs.

Malden lies dying. Rachel marries Louis and begins to experience
his dishonest ways. Julian who also pocketed funds from his aunt
confesses to Rachel and is forgiven. Louis confesses after an
accident which makes him fear death. Rachel at first will not
forgive him. Later a reconciliation occurs when she realizes that
she loves him enough to cope with his flaws.

Obviously, Bennett has constructed a plot that is very much
confined to one series of events involving few characters. His
central interest again is the husband-wife conflict. Because Rachel
has not the intelligence nor the spirit of Hilda Lessways, and Louis
has not the endurance nor the integrity of Edwin Clayhanger, the
reader, confined to their affairs, experiences a lack of significance
in the novel. Nevertheless, Bennett is working over material that
appears more importantly in *These Twain*. He weights the scales
differently in this marriage by making Rachel have a greater love
for her husband than he for her, and has the husband well aware of
his emotional advantage. In *These Twain* the principal figures are
very much in love with each other and equally vulnerable. Because
of the shallower natures of Rachel and Louis, and the more crude
form of the problem between them, Bennett denies himself scope
for the subtleties he develops so well in the later novel.

These Twain

Five years after the publication of *Hilda Lessways* Bennett
completed and published the last of the *Clayhanger* trilogy entitled
These Twain (1916).[17] The novel opens a few months after Edwin
and Hilda have married. From Edwin's nervousness that Hilda will
be late in coming to greet her guests at their first At Home party,
the chapters develop rising waves of crises in their relationship.
Every aspect of the novel serves in the delineation of the ebb and
flow of their disagr eements. Because the concentration in this
novel is on the two most vivid characters of the preceding two
novels in the trilogy, and because the focus is on the tensions in
their relationship, the emotional intensity so satisfyingly raised in
Clayhanger, then lost in *Hilda Lessways*, is raised again almost to
the level of the first novel.

Bennett organized the twenty chapters into three books cover-
ing the first three years of Edwin and Hilda's marriage. Each book
at a significant point in its arrangement includes a death or a

departure. At the end of book 1 the Orgreave parents die within twenty-four hours of each other leaving little but debts. Their marriage and their position at death represent irresponsible happiness to Edwin. At the end of book 2, George Cannon, having borrowed money from Edwin, leaves for America. Hilda's unsettled past is finally put behind them. In the penultimate chapter of book 3 Auntie Hamps dies and is buried. Her death clearly represents the removal of a pillar of conservatism, the end of an era. The final chapter, entitled "The Discovery," concludes with Edwin's reflections. The titles given each book are significant: Book 1, "The Woman in the House"; book 2 "The Past"; book 3 "Equilibrium." It becomes clear that Bennett develops a progression of discernment in Edwin. The emphasis is, as in *Clayhanger*, primarily upon the thoughts and feelings of the young man, although the reader frequently observes Hilda's positions.

In book 1 Edwin experiences a series of Hilda's independent actions which disturb him. He has had to bear her criticism that anyone could get the better of him in a land deal and she disapproves of the cost of proposed extensions to the shop. However, moments of communion occur. After Edwin has savagely put the living room back to his order and retired with a headache, he is surprised and thrilled by Hilda's ministrations and kisses. The book closes with the Orgreave deaths and Hilda reconciled to the extension of the shop.

Book 2 opens with Edwin proudly showing his relatives around the shop, but recognizing many instances of failure of courage in the new scheme of the works. He is aware that Hilda still thinks the changes too costly. When further calamity befalls Janet Orgreave and she must live with her sister in Dartmoor, Edwin is exercised over the fact that Hilda means to go with her for a time, and he fears that letters she has been receiving are from the imprisoned Cannon. Joining Hilda in Dartmoor, Edwin is appalled that a visit to the prison has been arranged. The shock of the visit effects a reconciliation between Edwin and Hilda. Later, Edwin generously helps Cannon to go to America.

Book 3 presents a restless Hilda at thirty-nine finding home and family insufficient employment. She wants to promote Edwin's position in the town. She also wants a larger home where she can organize a more fulfilling life. A problem with her son's eyes causes another crisis with Edwin as he wishes the boy to be treated

at home rather than in London. Hilda goes to London, nevertheless, having arranged for Edwin to stay with Auntie Hamps. While
he is there, Auntie Hamps sickens and dies. Sitting with her,
Edwin is forced to review his estimate of his aunt's life. An
accident to the bachelor Ingpen necessitates Edwin's going to
Ingpen's rooms to destroy personal papers for him. He finds a
woman sleeping there and has to review his estimate of Ingpen's
existence also. After Auntie Hamp's burial, the various experiences Edwin has had make him long for Hilda's return and he feels he
has gained insight into a woman's concerns. Upon her return, she
wants him to buy a dogcart which he willingly does and then she
proposes he buy a country estate. He stalks away to walk off his
instant anger. Coming to the bridge he had lingered upon when a
boy leaving school, he pauses until he concludes that there is no
good reason to deny Hilda's desires. Learning this, the enchanted
Hilda feels that "she was shaping the large contours of his
existence" and is "solemn in her bliss" (525). He is filled with the
sense of "the greatness of the adventure of existence with this
creature, to him unique, and the eternal expectation of some new
ecstasy, left no room in his heart for a regret" (525).

Readers who find *The Old Wives' Tale* more compelling, and
Clayhanger more essentially interesting than *These Twain*, might
consider that the differences in focus in the three books required
different feats of imagination in the author and demand differing
emphases in appreciation. In *The Old Wives' Tale* community
systems shape and trammel the lives of typical Five Towns
characters, and striking public events punctuate the narrative. In
Clayhanger the focus narrows as Bennett exorcises the ghosts of his
youth. In *These Twain* he concentrates upon the daily domesticities
of two common but distinctly different personalities. The ordinariness of everything in the book is accentuated beyond what we find
in *Anna of the Five Towns*, *The Old Wives' Tale*, and *Clayhanger*.

Some readers reject the reduction as the insignificant squab-
blings of an undistinguished couple submerged in the tawdry
materialistic pursuits of extending business premises and securing
larger homes. But it is Bennett's genius to take such intractable
material and, without investing it with any false glamor, provide
the perception of its extraordinariness to the individuals experiencing it, and the recognition of the important human truths

involved. Having established in *Clayhanger* Edwin's struggle to maintain his individuality; having established in *Hilda Lessways* Hilda's parallel struggle; and having established in both books the sources of mutual attraction and of potential difficulty between the two, Bennett, in *These Twain*, with remarkable sensitivity, delineates the causes and courses of clashes and truces as the couple move toward equilibrium.

Edwin, after long years of servitude, has an almost overpowering urge to be master in his own house. Hilda, after years of proud independence, cannot permit herself to dwindle into a docile wife. Edwin and Hilda both fear and despise spendthrift ways and wish to control money wisely, although differing widely in their notions of when to apply this control. Bennett concentrates upon these major sources of conflict.

From the synopsis of events, the structure clearly emerges. At the opening, Edwin both enjoys and fears Hilda's pervasion of his home. He has the psychological advantage of being established there, while Hilda has the psychological disadvantage of having to create her own space. Planning an At Home brings to the fore their very different approaches in organization. Edwin desires logic and order apart from any particular human needs; Hilda believes that human needs create new systems and require flexibility. The instances revealing this are worked into a pattern that begins with a fragile sense of togetherness in the success of the At Home and ends with a more certain sense of unity as they prepare to move to Ladderidge Hall. In between, three instances of alienation to one instance of reconciliation are worked into the remainder of book 1, and the same total in a varied arrangement is constructed in book 2. It is Edwin who must learn to adjust most. He comes to recognize that each of the instances of alienation were created more from the attitudes he harbored than from any inherent injustice in Hilda's behavior. He comes to acknowledge that, beyond the powerful sexual bond they share, there is much in her character that he honestly admires; that in her total person he does not wish to live without her. He perceives a courage in her to expand their horizons and finally exults in his willingness to give her rein to lead him. He can, with her, create a new joint space. In the end of the novel he is ready to give her a country estate, not as a yielding to the capriciousness of a woman, but as an agreement to move forward in anticipation into areas of greater natural happiness. This development in Edwin is traced through his encounters with all of the other characters.

The remaining characters are differentiated in terms of those who live by their systems and those who exist in their functions. Auntie Hamps is a vibrant creation of the stalwart Methodist reformer preserving an appearance of wealth and largesse, but living like a miser in her home. She asserts herself and her system, in a glorious overwhelming confidence, in a rustle of black silk and plumes, and the smell of leather in camphor, at all times insisting on the perfections of her family. Edwin finds her hypocritical and embarrassing; however, he cannot resist admiring the power of her presence and comes to recognize the validity of her love of family that gave meaning to her life. Ironically, it is she alone who shares with Edwin the category of choosing to live by a system.

The other family figures are realistically drawn individuals who have allowed themselves to be reduced to their functions. The pert, lively, shrewd child Clara has reduced herself as an adult to echoing her husband and mothering her children. Albert, her husband, is ambitious, but lacks the courage and wit to assert himself with integrity; he seeks recognition in holding petty offices in church and town. Maggie, the most reticent of the family, a capable manager with the courage to assert herself, has no ambition to rise above the level of housekeeper within the circle of her family. Hilda, so far removed from these figures in ability and ambition, suffers initially from Edwin's attempts to confine her to his system, and then to reduce her to a function. He does not perceive the bias of his attempts to influence Hilda, nevertheless instinctively draws away from the limitations of his family. Hilda's strength not only prevents her from being reduced to function, but also carries Edwin away from the narrowness of his system. That is the point at which the novel ends.

These Twain is a marvelously subtle book demonstrating that, in relationships, the strengths that one admires can be the source of unhappiness and alienation to others; that the weaknesses one despises can become the links, through compassion, binding disparate natures; that circumstances can maneuver one into viewing strengths as weaknesses, and weaknesses as strengths. The fact that these human truths can be demonstrated with humor and the presentation conclude in optimism provides another appealing dimension in the novel. The claim made for *Anna of the Five Towns* and for *The Old Wives' Tale* can be made for the *Clayhanger* trilogy, that the multiplicity of detail in depicting milieu, character, and event is artistically synthesized. With the completion of the trilogy, Bennett firmly established his maturity as an artist.

Chapter Six
Divided Interests

Following the completion of the *Clayhanger* trilogy, Bennett, as a frustrated civilian, sought avenues of service in the war effort. Directing his vast energies primarily into producing more than four hundred war articles and into committee work, he still continued producing novels, but, from 1915–1922, only those of his lighter sort: *The Lion's Share* (1916), *The Pretty Lady* (1918), *The Roll Call* (1919), *Lilian* (1922), and *Mr. Prohack* (1922). Within this period he separated from his wife. Not until *Riceyman Steps* (1923) do we find that involvement of writer with subject characteristic of Bennett's best work. However, he dashed off a sequel to *Riceyman Steps* called *Elsie and the Child* (1924). It does not approach the significance of its forerunner.

The Lion's Share

In the midst of disturbing preparations to visit the West Front, Bennett began in 1915 to write *The Lion's Share* as a serial for the *Strand Magazine*. At that stage, he said: "the novel is light, and of intent not deeply imagined, but it seems to me to be fairly good and interesting."[1] Its subject matter included suffragette scenes which eventually caused the *Strand* to refuse it. Returning from the front in July, he completed with difficulty the second half of the novel and had it accepted by the *Metropolitan* in New York and the *Grand Magazine* in London.

The novel features young, unconventional Audrey Moze who, upon the sudden deaths of her parents, is freed to leave her country home and go to Paris accompanied by the equally unconventional fifty-year-old Winnie Ingate. Having established these two characters as intelligent, unfettered, age-defying complementaries, and setting them toward London and Paris, Bennett is ready for a gambol into the haunts of artists and the idle wealthy in the two sophisticated cities he knew well. The plot is as much a "frolic" as the plots in his novels given that subtitle. But Bennett includes, beside comedy, authentic milieu well rendered, timely issues, and characterizations capturing his personal concerns. It is an unusual, uneven amalgam.

In Paris Audrey and Winnie meet Tommy and Nick, two American artist-hopefuls, and Musa, a French violinist, in whose company they attend a masquerade at an established artist's studio. All the exaggerations of the jet set of the time are animatedly captured by Bennett as Audrey begins her education in Continental sophistication. In six months she is proficient in French and Winnie is progressing in painting. At home on the Left Bank, Audrey decides to taste the luxuries of the Right Bank and pursue her interest in Musa. Hearing that Nick had sustained an injury in a suffragette struggle in London, she returns there to help the Cause.

Up to this point, Bennett's treatment of character and setting is reasonably substantial and interesting. He captures the frenetic world of Parisian Left Bank cafés, studios, salons, with the appreciation of the habitué, yet carefully distinguishes the viewpoint of the eager, young, English country-girl attempting to maintain equilibrium. From Audrey's return to the suffragettes in London, however, Bennett thrusts her into a cops-and-criminals chase which includes many farcical situations. Finally, Audrey hides at the home of the Spatts, a London couple living in an east coast village. Bennett obviously enjoys satirizing the Spatts as incompetent snobs fancying themselves reformers for sheltering suffragettes and arrogant German nationals whom they try unsuccessfully to patronize.

The Paris and London episodes are linked when Nick comes to the Spatts with Musa. Suddenly, Audrey is jealous, and this produces the final coils of action which conclude the novel with her marriage to the French violinist. Audrey rejects a political refugee's monomania for suffragettism, she rejects a French woman's ideal of her own Continental marriage, and declares she will be the "new" woman with husband and with cause in reasonable perspective.

Recent criticism of the novel tends to raise its merit somewhat. Kinley E. Roby, in 1972, found the story "well told, and—at least in the first half—brimming with life."[2] John Lucas, in 1974, identified the flaws resulting from mixed intentions, but commended the novel's comic complement as "perhaps the best broad comedy that Bennett ever wrote."[3] Margaret Drabble, in 1974, found the novel "in many ways a good read and a pure escape for both reader and writer."[4] For the critics who reject what they feel is Bennett's trifling with serious issues, he states that he was not planning to proselytize, but merely to describe "the livest and the most generally interesting scenes of modern life." The novel was to present "a young girl finding her beliefs and her ways in life." It was to be "mainly occupied with the affections."[5] Bennett would expect his emphasis to be appreciated. But his treatment of his chosen material lacks coherence and provides no depth.

The Roll Call

As early as 1911 Bennett had planned to write a history of Hilda Lessway's son to be published in 1914.[6] He did not, in fact, begin to write it until 1916, then wrote *The Pretty Lady* and published that, before his account of George Cannon, entitled *The Roll Call*, found a publisher in 1919.

The novel begins in 1901 with George Cannon as the young protégé of Enwright, the eccentric senior member of a firm of architects. He courts their clerk's gentle daughter, but breaks their engagement when she feels obliged to care for her widowed father. He becomes interested in a more vivacious girl who lives with her parents in Paris. She encourages him in his work. He wins a competition for design of a northern town hall, following which he marries the girl. After ten years of marriage, with the expected addition of a third child, George decides he must enlist in the army and leave his family to the care of his stepfather Edwin Clayhanger. The novel ends with his sense of exultation as, having no longer any individual responsibility except to obey commands, he lies with the troops fatigued in the rain at a campsite on their first maneuver.

The novel is negligible. Its plot drags, its characterization is undistinguished, its language often trite. Nothing has significance except for the fact that Bennett in this novel is saying farewell to his Five Towns people and his past, and is taking up London people and the present. As the first of his "war novels" (his phrase), it merely presents a superficial patriotism at the end. Yet there are some good things in it. Bennett captures the zeal of the promising young architect. He gives an interesting brief portrait of Agnes, a Chelsea artist with lesbian tendencies. He includes an impressive scene when George enters the cavernous structure of the great Westminster Cathedral and sees its dying architect, Bentley, looking longingly over his half-realized dream. He allows George and Marguerite one well-rendered scene—the breaking of their engagement. He briefly, but effectively, suggests the dazzling effects on the young of the provincial Spring parade of Paris fashions at the races. He sympathetically projects the state of the terminally pregnant Lois. He captures the enlisted soldier's sense of disorientation as he is engulfed in military red tape. Nevertheless, the novel strikes this reader as the most perfunctory treatment of material Bennett ever offered as serious fiction.

The Pretty Lady

"The chief thing yesterday was that I began on my novel about the French cocotte, with gusto,"[7] wrote Bennett, May 25, 1917. His *Journal* entries indicate that in contrast to the writing of *The Roll Call*, the writing of *The Pretty Lady* continued steadily until its completion January 28, 1918, when he noted his complete satisfaction with its close. Its publication in the spring brought charges of pornography from reviewers and threats of litigation from the Catholic Federation; it was banned from the stalls of Boots and W. H. Smith. The publicity sent its sales to thirty thousand copies in England by September. His confidence in the novel received some unusual support. George Moore pronounced Christine "the finest cocotte in literature";[8] and Lord Beaverbrook, believing the novel showed Bennett's remarkable insight into French psychology, invited Bennett to join him in the Ministry of Information as director of British propaganda in France.[9] Bennett believed that he "could tell practically everything"[10] about the existence of a professional French courtesan and planned to place her in a war novel.

Bennett concentrates upon four characters, the middle-aged G. J. Hoape, and the three women who attract him, Concepcion Smith, Lady Queenie Paulle, both society ladies, and Christine Dubois, a French prostitute. Concepcion and Queenie are driven to extremes of behavior by the war. Christine is mainly oblivious to it no matter how many signs of it she sees. G. J. denies the war has begun at first, then guiltily, but dully, seeks some service. Eventually, he gains experience and understanding, ceases to be a wealthy dilettante, and acquires stature as a responsible citizen. Concern and commonsense characterize basically both G. J. and Concepcion. At the novel's end their future together is suggested.

Christine is presented as wholly committed to her trade, viewing it as a service for which she is naturally talented. She views her assets practically and carefully plans for her eventual retirement. Bennett slowly reveals Christine's superstitious one-track existence and makes her entirely believable, although the presentation is marred by the absurdities of her literally translated language.

The construction of events illuminates Bennett's view of London characters caught in the national conflict. Queenie and Concepcion, highly strung thoroughbreds of a type fascinating to Bennett, take typical, but differing paths in their response to social crisis. Queenie, thought to be modeled upon Beaverbrook's friend, Diana Manners,[11] is well done. She enjoys being a *femme fatale* and haughtily assumes deference from all. But, in spite of her cynical intelligence, she throws herself into almost useless fund-raising activities typical of her class. As she shares the sorrows of Concepcion, in the midst of increasing horrors in London, her control gives way. Only a mad excitement experienced in the danger of being on the rooftop in a blitz can lift her out of the futility of her existence. She courts death.

Concepcion's personality is similar to Queenie's, but she is more balanced. She chooses a very practical way to serve in the war effort. But, in carrying out her duties and in an attempt to forget her young husband's death, she overworks. When she witnesses a horrible accident in the factory as one of the girls has her hair caught in the machinery, is scalped, and bleeds to death, Concepcion's control also gives way. She leaves the factory and experiences a loss of purpose which eventually brings her to contemplating suicide. Because she tells Hoape of her plan, because she has reached out to him before, it is clear that she, too, is in love with him. Bennett's tracing of an intelligent, strong young woman's breakdown into despair is effectively disturbing.

He is less successful in delineating Hoape. In contrast to the distinct and believable presentations of the women, the major male figure is not distinct. The women know what they know and are definite in action. Hoape is seeking certitudes, yet tends to avoid definite action. The result is that the vagueness in his mind becomes a vagueness in his presentation. It is interesting to note how many unflattering details true of Bennett himself are included in his portrait of Hoape. He is capable of mocking himself over his taste for the heavily opulent in furniture, of his need to account for every penny spent, of his demanding punctuality of associates, of his dislike of some extreme forms of interior decoration in vogue among moderns like the founders of the Omega Workshop. But he allows himself no flattery in the portrait. Hoape remains generally unattractive, a collection of traits more than a coherent characterization.

It is easy to see, however, why the book would appeal to many readers of the time. Apart from the shocking central relationship, Bennett manages to include almost every controversial aspect of the war. The confusion and unnecessary loss of life among refugees in Continental ports, the conflicting directions from the War Office, the stupidity on the battlefield, complacency and indifference at home, abuse of the press, futility of the wealthy, condition of soldiers back from the front on leave, class prejudices, all receive pointed presentation. Within almost each area of concern Bennett includes an image of horror. In Christine's account of Ostend a mother and baby sit with arms perforated by the same bullet; in an exclusive St. James's shoe shop a pale parody of a man is stamped underground; in the soldier's account the calvary ride over a still living but fallen comrade who dies later; in the narrator's account of the fashionable at an art exhibition is included the comment that the well-dressed viewers are helping pay for hospitals where, at the moment of their viewing, dissevered legs and arms were being thrown into buckets; in Concepcion's account a young girl is scalped by factory machinery; in G. J.'s attempt to locate his walking stick in an air raid he finds a child's severed arm with bits of a dress clinging to it and a small ring still on one of the fingers. The disturbing images, increasing in horror, emphasize the brutality of war in specific personal terms.

It is only when G. J. ceases to wish for a selfish "surcease" from a vague sense of doom, becomes directly involved in work that carries him to the front and begins to make him a power at home, that he appears to gain a confidence Concepcion notices. That confidence allows him to take on the challenge of a relationship with Concepcion and plan to use his powers to the full in more war work until the horrors are overcome. The novel is Bennett's look into the abyss, but his conclusion leaves room for hope, reminding one that that syllable is the name given to the main figure.

Mr. Prohack and Lilian

Both *Mr. Prohack* and *Lilian* were published in 1922. The first novel was begun in 1920 and finished in 1921, but the second novel was dashed off in two months, December, 1921—January, 1922. Neither novel approaches serious art; however, *Mr. Prohack* is a better book than *Lilian*. Mr. Prohack is a variation of the Henry Machin type and Lilian is another old man's darling who gains legal security. Prohack is obviously shaped to allow Bennett outlet for the quips and outrageous attitudes he enjoyed indulging. Prohack, more than twenty years "the terror of the departments" within the Treasury, finds his postwar economic position difficult until he discovers he is heir to a fortune from a man he had helped years before. The rest of the novel presents how he, his wife, daughter, and son react to the windfall.

Prohack has one dimension, the confident humorist given to ironic preachments, usually in control of events, preserving a crusty surface that hides from none his basic benevolence. This gives the tone of the book. Either you are prepared to follow another "frolic" in his company, or you may find the treatment irritating. The other characters are shown providing Prohack with opportunities to display his eccentricities. When his wife wants a car and larger home, he puffs and bluffs that he prefers the simple life, causes all manner of exasperating delays in her schemes, all the while enjoying the expansion of their material pleasures. The plot is filled with farcical situations; Bennett's ingenuity seems inexhaustible. Prohack's function would appear to be to identify human inanities and, in his facetious way, cut out cant.

Lilian scarcely deserves describing except as a journeyman's job carried through. The girl of the title is left orphaned by a father who adored her, but did nothing to secure her future. She has notions of a good life, and knows she cannot achieve it working at a typing agency. When circumstances bring the owner of the agency to the offices as she is doing her late-night duty, she proceeds to charm him, becomes his mistress, travels to the Continent with him, becomes pregnant, nurses him in a bout of pneumonia, marries him just before he dies of the disease, returns to the agency as employer, and retires to his home to devote herself to rearing his heir. None of the characters are more than types. Nothing in the plot is made significant. There is no complement of Bennett humor. The speed of the composition of the novel indicates Bennett's lack of involvement. In fact, the swift progress of the work is all Bennett notes of this book in his journal or letters.

Riceyman Steps and *Elsie and the Child*

Following the breakdown of his marriage and legal separation from Marguerite, Bennett in 1922 met and fell in love with Dorothy Cheston, the beautiful young actress with whom he spent the rest of his life. In perhaps his happiest period he produced *Riceyman Steps*, which, upon its publication in 1923, brought him instant acclaim and the award from Edinburgh University of the James Tait Black Memorial Prize for the best novel of that year. Its sequel, *Elsie and the Child*, followed in the next year, but it is not equal in merit.

Bennett worked upon far more intractable material in *Riceyman Steps* than any he had previously used in his best work. With Richard Larch, Anna, Constance and Sophia, Edwin and Hilda, Bennett had the always interesting period of youth to present, the stirring of ambitions, the emotions of young love to delineate. He had set their stories primarily in the Potteries he knew and could render well. But, for *Riceyman Steps*, he chose Henry Earlforward, past forty and a miser; Violet Arb, fortyish and a nervous widow; Elsie Sprickett, stolid, simple, twenty-three, and a servant; set them in the grimy environs of Clerkenwell, east central London, and gave little more than a year of their daily lives for the plot. Any brief synopsis of the tale can only suggest its ordinariness, if not its tawdriness. Yet to read the novel is to experience a power in writing that unquestionably vindicates Bennett's impressionistic genius.

It is a strangely moving presentation. Bennett forces the reader to have an almost overwhelming awareness of significant mystery in living and demonstrates that that awareness is present to the most limited intelligence. The values in relationships are to be understood by very different signs than those offered by any of his contemporaries or any who had written novels before him. The impulse to show love by generosity, the impulse to appear well in the eyes of the beloved, the admiration for strength coupled with a terrible anxiety for the form that strength takes, the compromise with idiosyncrasies, the clash of individualities, the understandings of the inarticulate, all are revealed with remarkable sensitivity and sympathy through surface simplicities, gaining a cumulative power difficult to illustrate adequately.

As with all of his best novels, Bennett divides his material into significant blocks, giving this novel five major units. Part 1 presents the old bookshop, the courtship of Henry and Violet and lovers' meetings of Elsie with her shell-shocked boyfriend, Joe. Part 2 covers the days of the wedding period for Henry and Violet. Part 3 delineates a day, almost a year later, in the lives of the three major figures. Part 4 develops a crisis ending wih Violet's departure to hospital. In parts 2, 3 and 4 Joe has been sent away and Elsie sees nothing of him. Then, part 5 brings Violet's death, the final crisis for Henry, followed by his death, a crisis for Joe restoring him to Elsie's care, and the dissolution of the bookshop. The parts readily fit the dramatic pattern of introduction, complication, climax, resolution, dénouement. After the great struggle in *Riceyman Steps* comes the haunting sense of transience. Even though the final view is that of Elsie and Joe, now husband and wife, walking away from the desolation of the bookstore to their new home, much of the imagery of the last chapter casts around the lives of both couples echoes of that ancient biblical statement ending: "and the wind passeth over it and it is gone."

Bennett achieves an admirable feat in the creation of the miser Henry Earlforward. Immediately introduced, Henry is briefly and carefully described as having "vitality," as giving "an appearance of quiet, intelligent, refined and kindly prosperity."[12] He has the near-sighted brown eyes and passion for gold of George Eliot's famous miser. But Bennett requires of Henry no loss of his hoard, nor loss of his obsession, in order for the reader to appreciate the man's humanity. Bennett causes Henry to give way to his demon in an increasingly terrible way that leads directly to his death, and to the death of his wife, yet makes the reader ever appeciative of his "intelligent," "refined," "kindly" personality, and even wryly admiring of his formidable fortitude. He literally starves and freezes himself and his wife to death; nevertheless their love for each other is made entirely credible and moving. The effect of the opening description is to attract the reader to a mature, settled man, comfortable to know.

Bennett next sets the scene of the Steps which connect Kings' Cross Road with the higher ground of the Square behind it. In a little cul-de-sac, a few houses, a few stores, among them Violet's confectioners' shop and Henry's secondhand bookstore, can be seen from the Steps. This is not St. Luke's Square transferred to London. Bennett imaginatively realizes the area and people of Clerkenwell in a way he had only achieved before in descriptions of the Five Towns.

As Henry pauses on the Steps to look at Violet's shop, his mind flits to Clerkenwell in the Middle Ages when all was pastoral and mystery plays were performed there; he imagines some of the present architecture suggests still the buttressed walls of fortresses. These details might seem negligible, but they have multiple significance. In his best works Bennett writes with a concentration of meaning not always appreciated. In *Riceyman Steps* the concentration is greater than in any of his other serious fiction. There are only three major figures, the limited sphere of the Steps for action, with some days of one year for time. Then, the symbolism is more pervasive and coherent than in any previous work. Finally, all details carry layers of information, as do the details given above. Those indicate Henry's erudition, his imaginative, romantic turn of mind, and they suggest one source of Henry's later rationalizations of his eccentricities. He would be very familiar with the habits of holy men and with the ancient values of fasting. The image of the enclosed fortress also significantly recurs.

Henry limps down the Steps to follow a customer into his shop. Bennett begins to accumulate unobtrusively details that gradually identify the psychological crippling of which the physical impairment is an outward sign. The customer is Dr. Raste who practices medicine in the neighboring Square. He pretends to want a book of Shakespeare, but really wants to ask about Elsie after whom his shell-shocked patient Joe is running madly. As Henry searches for the book, the shop is described. The dust and disarray beyond the first few tidy shelves would attract a bibliophile, but Bennett writes: "The effect was of mysterious and vast populations of books imprisoned forever in everlasting shade, chained, deprived of air and sun and movement, hopeless, resigned, martyrized" (6). Every part of this description comes to be appropriate to the condition of the residents of the house above the shop. By the end of chapter 3 Bennett has established Henry's significant character traits which determine the course of events. His confident, unperturbable, procrastinating ways, his genuine kindliness, joined to his obsession, make of his character an immovable force that bears Violet down.

Violet Arb is admirably created also. Her bargaining over a cookbook so delights Henry that he struggles with himself and gives her the book. All her movements are quick and pleasing, she has opinions of her own, and her laughter delights him. Her brief history is that of the lively wife of a much-traveled, equally lively, clerk of works who died leaving her a considerable legacy but no permanent home. Inheriting the shop in Riceyman Steps, she seized upon it as an outlet for her energy and a way to keep her finances secure. Bennett writes:

> She had, nevertheless, a cancer—not a physical one: the secret abiding terror lest despite all her outward appearance she might be incapable of managing her possessions. . . . She had a vision . . . of herself in poverty and solitude. (27)

This fear helps her look favorably upon Henry when later he comes courting, just as Henry's fear of losing Elsie's services when she marries Joe gives impetus to his courting of Violet. In this novel the connections are drawn so close that the sense of an irresistible tide powerfully affects the reader. The use of the term "cancer" above might strike the reader as odd. It is indeed a more obtrusive example of Bennett's intention to include only details having links throughout the narrative. Henry dies of a cancer of the gullet; Violet dies of a fibrous growth in the womb, both conditions aggravated beyond help by their starved condition.

Violet's joyful entry upon married life with Henry, then the total loss of that joy without the loss of the love she feels for him, is movingly developed. In part 2 Bennett shapes travesties of a wedding, the exchange of gifts and a honeymoon. Throughout the day Henry's love for Violet is reinforced in many ways, but his penurious mind is disturbed. Arriving home, Henry is appalled to find that Violet's wedding gift is a commercial vacuuming of his filthy shop. He, in turn, gives her an old safe he had bought just for her private things. She is shocked. The whole wedding episode sounds farcical. But Bennett does not mock these people. He lets us view the exterior absurd, but carefully presents their interior logic.

Elsie, a young widow, becomes resident maid and is given a room upstairs. Her employers know nothing more of her relationship with Joe than that she had parted from him after he had brandished a knife at Violet when he had been angered at Elsie's staying to help Violet on his birthday. They do not comprehend Elsie. Bennett in the servant shapes a life force more powerful, more positive, than that animating either Henry or Violet. Her reactions have the primitive power combined with the great dignity of a votaress of ancient time. In fact, she is referred to as a goddess, then a priestess, at appropriate places in the novel. Her power stems from her great instinct to serve. She cares little for possessions, having never had any. Her great passion is for Joe.

Bennett constructs an unusual love scene in which Elsie runs in the rain from Violet's shop to Joe who has been waiting in a corner under an umbrella. She steps under the umbrella necessarily resting her body against his. He encircles her waist with his free arm. When Joe despairs because she cannot go with him, Elsie takes the umbrella and directs him to hold her tight with both arms. He cannot argue, but clasps her fiercely. Bennett writes: "She kissed him, keeping her lips on his. She kissed him until she knew from the feel of his muscles everywhere that the warm soft contact with her had begun to dissolve his resentment" (31). Her unselfconscious, natural, warm responses have a healing power.

But she is not immune to troubles. After awaiting Joe's return for many months, she begins to despair and develops a ravenous appetite. As her employers eat less and turn away food, she keeps eating even the scraps and comes to raid the larder. As the Earlforwards become obsessed with their conditions and less able to dominate Elsie, she, needing involvement of some kind, becomes temporarily obsessed, too. However, her obsession is not the negation of sustenance, but its opposite. When Joe eventually staggers back to the shop in a malarial fever, Elsie hides him in her room and cares for him assiduously, losing all her urge to overeat. The frightful folly of the older couple is ironically counterpointed with the fundamental wisdom of the younger couple.

Bennett concentrates the climax into the morning, afternoon, and evening of one day. He creates the sense of an approaching turning point by having Violet stage a campaign to persuade Henry to eat an egg for breakfast and a steak for dinner. That life-and-death issues are involved no reader can ignore. Failing in her campaign, Violet rages out all the truths of their situation as she sees it. Henry's response early and late is a bland reply and a silent departure. Violet capitulates, seeks him out, and they solemnize their reunion by sharing with each other knowledge of what is protected in each other's safe. Violet, reconciled to Henry, hopes against hope that the strength of his character will save them both. The whole of part 3 is well done.

Part 4 documents and dramatizes the stages of the Earlforwards' breakdown, with more and more desperate measures attempted to prevent the worst from happening. It is Elsie who understands and takes the only steps possible. With sure instinct she says they need someone from outside. Her stress on the words makes the enormity of the sealed and suffocating house clear to Violet, but she does not agree to the ruse of fetching the doctor to see her. Elsie fetches the doctor without permission. From his coming, events occur swiftly. Henry takes to his bed to frighten Elsie from thieving food, but he never leaves his bed again until the day of his death. Violet, sensing her own serious illness, tries to force Henry to agree to go to the hospital. Their battle of wills in the shadowed bedroom within the silent dust-laden house is well done. But it is Violet who is carried away.

Part 5 traces with clinical accuracy the final stages of deterioration in Henry Earlforward, featuring the moments of luminous clarity, the racing thoughts, the ill will and suspicion of the terribly sick, and the last heroic effort to return to work and deny death characteristic of the formidable force of this man. After Joe returns in a malarial fever and is hidden upstairs, the tensions developed are those of Elsie's efforts to tend Joe properly while disarming the suspicions aroused in the extrasensitive, dying old man. How she copes with her new responsibilities, accepts authority, and gains the respect of Dr. Raste and his small daughter are caught in brief episodes and long meditative passages emphasizing the sense of strength she engenders by simple acceptance.

Bennett's fascination with the significance of exceedingly simple things, with the far-reaching and sometimes extreme consequences of slight degrees of difference within similarities, shapes the meaning of *Riceyman Steps*. He gives to Henry vitality, to Violet energy. He makes Elsie hardworking. However, Henry's vitality is distinguished as mental strength; Violet's energy is distinguished as the need for physical activity. Only Elsie has abounding physical strength. Henry is characterized by placidity, patience, procrastination. Elsie is always anxious but instinctively accepting. Joe desires but is incapable of initiating change. On the surface these people would appear very similar among the enduring respectable poor. But the changes Bennett rings on the operation of these characteristics, within the individuals and upon each other, produce striking polarities in results. The characteristics cited above are all acceptable and understandable. All of these people are basically kind. Each couple shares mutual love. Then, Bennett gives the extreme trait of miserliness to one of the four figures in combination with a powerful will, and the reader perceives that although both loves are strong and complete, the love of the older wealthy couple actually permits their problem to grow, while the love of the very poor younger couple allows them to see no problems at all. Bennett's careful structure is aimed at the recognition of enigmas in volition.

The great popularity of Elsie, although it annoyed him at the time,[13] led Bennett in 1924 to write a sequel devoted to her life with Joe and her relationship with Dr. Raste's young daughter Eva. *Elsie and the Child* is short, having only ten chapters, and is obviously merely an attempt to ride on the tide of the excellent sales of *Riceyman Steps*. Bennett is always competent in shaping a plot and filling it out with appropriate incident. But this tale is simply the elaboration of one event—the decision to send Eva to boarding school.

It opens with Elsie attempting to carry out her ambition to wait on table as Joe contentedly spends his time in the kitchen as cook. While serving dinner, she is aware of Eva's unhappiness in the presence of a lady guest, the headmistress of a school in Bournemouth where Eva is to go. Eva's difficulty is that she feels she can leave her parents but cannot bear to part with Elsie. Elsie's response is to suggest that she and Joe should leave their employment with the Rastes because of their daughter's disloyalty. Joe's reaction is to erupt into the violence always latent in his shell-shocked state as he considers the possibility of having to leave his sanctuary. It is his angry statements to Eva that convince her she will lose Elsie altogether if she does not go sensibly to school. The tale ends as she is being driven to the train station. There is nothing new added to the dimensions of those characters met in *Riceyman Steps*, and nothing else of significance is developed. The tone is sentimental.

In retrospect, this period can be seen to include a significant turning point for Bennett. The long years of the Great War and its aftermath deflected Bennett's interests in novel writing for a time into superficial treatments of current events or current modes of behavior. In these books the transition from Five Towns to London occurs naturally, but because of the quality of most of these books, the importance of the change is scarcely to be noted. However, *Riceyman Steps* triumphantly demonstrates that what drew his artist's eye in the Potteries is no less likely to be found in London, or anywhere else. Regionalism does not apply. Certain human traits drew his careful study again and again. In Henry Earlforward an invincible certitude is frighteningly exposed. In Bennett's next important London novel the opposite characteristic is powerfully traced.

Chapter Seven
Last Years

The remaining six years of Bennett's life were the most crowded. The period as recorded in *Journals* and *Letters* included intervals of amazing good health, domesticity encompassing the surprising advent of a daughter, immersion in theatrical activity, increased output of journalism and occasional pieces, a social round of incredible proportions, extensive travel, and the production of five complete novels, with a sixth left unfinished at his death. Two of the novels, *Lord Raingo* (1926) and *Imperial Palace* (1930), are impressive; the rest, *The Strange Vanguard* (1927), *Accident* (1928), *Venus Rising From the Sea* (1932), and the fragment *Dream of Destiny* (1932), are mainly on the level of his fantasies.

Lord Raingo

In *Lord Raingo* Bennett creates a powerful study of an intelligent, sensitive, benevolent middle-aged man, confident in his commercial enterprise, shrewd in politics, but suffering from class inferiority and sexual insecurity. The novel begins at the point in Raingo's life when he is seeking some new world to conquer. He has failed as a member of the House of Commons because he lacks any skill in oratory, but is still keenly interested in the political maneuvers of the party in power under Andy Clyth. He follows the progress of the war, learns that his only son Geoffrey is held prisoner in Germany, and feels the futility of an over-aged citizen who needs action. He never forgets that for all his millions he was not born to the class of gentleman. His wife Adela is an aristocrat whom he no longer loves. For a relatively brief time he has been keeping a mistress, Delphine, in rooms in London.

From this opening situation, the plot would appear to emphasize Raingo's new career in politics until illness and death overtake him. It is true that two thirds of the book, constituting part 1, present his actions as new Minister of Records, and all of the remaining third, constituting part 2, present the astonishing tour de force of Raingo's dying. But woven throughout the whole is his problem with Delphine, and behind that, the essential problem of his eroding sense of inferiority.

The note is struck in the first paragraph. Bennett writes of Raingo: "Not by taking any amount of thought can you become a country gentleman."[1] Raingo gazes over Mozewater, watching the tide creep over dangerous sands. Echoing Matthew Arnold, a poet Bennett admired, Raingo recognizes that the ebb and flow "drew him out of his own melancholy and futility into a melancholy and futility greater, grander, and far more beautiful." As the novel proceeds, Raingo, with few moments of respite, fights his fears and his melancholia. It is part of the ironic construction that Raingo sees melancholia as the most serious flaw in his beloved Delphine's personality, but does not recognize its serious presence in himself. The chapter ends with Raingo wistfully asking the village doctor how long he has to live, and Heddle's responding that he could live twenty years if he takes care of his heart and avoids catching a disease like pneumonia. The novel traces how, in fact, Raingo abuses his heart, and it ends with his death in only a year from complications of pneumonia.

Adela remains the enigma her husband believes her to be, for the omniscient narrator gives only Raingo's view of her. Raingo's thoughts in chapter 2 include these significant musings: "But herself, she had style and dignity and carriage. . . . She had race. He hadn't. He did not quite know why she married him." His insecurities are clear. Delphine is more fully developed, but also presented only from Raingo's view. His suspicions that she is unfaithful to him are constant. Upon the occasion when he fears she is hiding a young man in her bedroom and it proves to be her younger sister, Bennett writes: "For a few moments Sam dared not attempt to speak, lest he should sob—yes, sob—and he averted his eyes that Delphine might not see the wet shine on them" (19). This may sound like sentimental trash. And Raingo is a sentimental man. But the frequency of his struggling with tears on both public and private occasions, draws attention to his deep-seated malaise. The nearness of tears is a clear medical symptom of mental fatigue and depression, as Geoffrey points out to his father in part 2.

Wanting to be "something more than a mere millionaire" (21) accounts for most of Raingo's actions for the remainder of part 1.

Bennett expertly handles Raingo's brief career in politics. He had carefully vetted all the material with Lord Beaverbrook. Rumor that Bennett's politicians could be readily identified greatly increased interest in the novel's publication. Andy Clyth has been identified as Lloyd George, Tom Hogarth as Winston Churchill, Lord Ochleford as Lord Milner, and Hasper Clews as Bonar Law. Raingo himself was believed to be modeled upon Lord Rhondda.[2] But Bennett's imaginative grasp of the material produces an interest with values far beyond a flurry of local identification. The subtle thrust and parry in the unceasing contest between potentially jarring personalities to maintain or improve their individual political positions in the Cabinet is engrossing. The presentation is fresh and includes group humor that makes these episodes the brightest and most vital in the book. The viewpoint is mainly Raingo's. His moments of luck, of surprise, of struggling for buoyancy in the sea of intrigue, account for some of the freshness. The lively dialogue quickly suggesting the personalities of the others completes the successful combination.

Alternating with chapters of temporarily successful political activity are chapters of unsuccessful personal life. Raingo discovers Adela cares little for his gaining a peerage. Going to his club and seeing Delphine with a young soldier there, his sensations frighten him, but he thinks he "must take hold of himself, drag himself out of this slough of vile morbidity into which he had weakly and odiously slipped" (105). Then political problems develop. His activities in the press bring Cabinet criticism; his outmaneuvering of a distinguished colonel will bring an attack on Raingo necessitating his making a speech in the House. The strains of the ceremony of his elevation to the peerage, his presentation to the King, the shock of Adela's accidental death, her very public funeral, the return of his emaciated son, his ordeal in the House, prove a killing combination. The ebb and flow of Raingo's uncertainties, the alternations of public and private crises, are linked in these chapters by a complex interplay of one set of his fears upon the other. The combination is masterly.

Part 2 opens with Raingo being sent home to Moze Hall and persuaded into bed. For twenty-seven chapters Bennett details the progress of his dying. It is powerful and strange. Of all the deaths in Bennett's novels this one is the most prolonged and gains in effect because the viewpoint is Raingo's. The authenticity of the medical facts was approved by Bennett's own doctor. Part 2 fulfills Bennett's intention of doing a death "on a magnificent scale."[3]

Within the plotting of the stages of decline, the same exterior-interior, public-private juxtapositions of the battle of Raingo's life are maintained. The arena is now confined to his bedroom. All the significant people eventually turn up there. The process is again the preservation of his determined, game facade to the figures in his public life, and the growth of depression in his interior life until the final crisis.

In the chapter significantly entitled "The Will to Win" he learns from Gwen that the tears she and Delphine had earlier shed were indeed, as he suspected, for a young soldier's unhappiness. He is told he now has pneumonia in both lungs and will reach a crisis in one week. As he slips in and out of delirium, he feels more terribly alone. By chance, in a newspaper full of his illness, he reads of a suicide at Brighton and *knows* it is Delphine. He is told she felt responsible for the soldier's death and felt Raingo would never marry an appropriate wife while she lived. Finally, when death is near, Gwen comes with an enlarged picture of Delphine which she puts at the foot of his bed. He becomes fully conscious to gaze at it as the lights grow dimmer. His former gardener, now an enlisted soldier, needing desperately to do something, gets the generators going, and Raingo dies in a blaze of lights calling the name of Adela.

That it should be his wife's name strikes some readers as odd and ambiguous. But on three occasions in the novel Bennett has Raingo feel disturbed over similarities in the two women: when he reflects upon their lack of ambition, when he realizes that both addressed him in exactly the same terms after being told of his peerage, when, having given up his ambition that Adela might rise to the requirements of the position of Lady Raingo, he finds himself in even greater distress having to give up the same ambition for Delphine. His attempts to be fair in mind even to his enemies leave him again and again with a sense of guilt about Adela. With Delphine's picture at his feet and a vision of her resting against him, it is not psychologically false that he should cry out his wife's name at the end.

The novel is not an unflawed structure. Although Bennett's imaginative control of the long dying process is remarkable indeed, its length is arbitrary in the total scheme of the book. The women lack the clear definition of the men. The text includes phrasing that leaves one uneasy. Repetitions of words like "miraculous," "majestic," "summit of life," "romantic," "formidable," statements like "his illness was marvellous, and in its terror and grandeur it was the most marvellous thing that had ever happened to him" (336), leave one with the uncomfortable feeling that Bennett is striving to capture special significance but falling into meaningless superlatives.

There is nevertheless greatness in Bennett's careful presentation of the deteriorating power of a destructive state of mind. By keeping mainly to Raingo's viewpoint we can more sympathetically realize the man's struggles to overcome his tendency to feel insecure, to fear the worst, out of which the depression increasingly grows. But nothing can stand before it, neither political success, status, the love of Delphine, nor his physical strength. The mental tide is given its correlative in images of the sea which recur with terrible point in the text. Raingo's gloom is increased as he watches the sea at the novel's opening, he is described as a struggling swimmer far from shore in his political crisis midway in the book, and he literally drowns in his own blood at the end. One can sense something of the fear Bennett experienced as he explored a human malaise he sometimes suffered from himself.

The Strange Vanguard and *Accident*

Bennett sets the level of *The Strange Vanguard* quite clearly in his Journal entry for June 10, 1926. It is no more than "a fantastic lark, nor pretends to be more,"[4] he says. He indicates more substance for *Accident* in an October 30 entry in the same year:

I had already got the moral background for it: the dissatisfaction of a successful and rich man with his own secret state of discontent and with the evils of the age. I wanted a frame. . . . I suddenly thought that I would extend the rôle of the *train de luxe*, . . . to be the scene of the whole of the novel—so that the entire time-space of the novel will only be about thirty hours or so.[5]

Bennett's notion of having a lark in *The Strange Vanguard* is positively puckish. It would appear as if he thought that all the most unlikely settings and most outlandish actions along the course of the most unbelievable plot-line would indeed be a joke for the reading public. It is a fairy tale in the absurd.

It is set up as a mystery. First a tycoon, Septimius Sutherland, finds his hotel services ceased because of a strike. Another guest, Count Veruda, invites the guests to dine on his yacht. After dining, all but Sutherland and young Harriet Perkins are taken to shore. The remaining two find the ship sailing away with them when they come up on deck from having explored the engine room. The boat is actually owned by Lord Furber, another speculator, who had Veruda plan the hotel strike in order to kidnap Sutherland temporarily to force him to sell his shares in a company Furber wants.

Harriet is a flippant, clever adventuress who knows Furber's wife. She attracts the urbane Sutherland, manages the choleric Furber with her audacity, and plays the vamp with ship's personnel. All sorts of ridiculous situations are developed out of these combinations. Eventually, they dock near Rome. Then Sutherland and Furber have discussions on the wall of the Coliseum and at the very top of the dome of St. Peter's, but Furber doesn't get the shares. They sail to Monte Carlo to gamble on them and there Furber's estranged wife turns up. They are reconciled when it becomes clear that Furber wanted to own the company to which his wife owed a dress bill in order that he could conclude a quarrel with her over nonpayment and not lose face. Nothing could be more farfetched.

In *Accident* Alan Frith-Walter is an educated, cultured business-man whose wealth was inherited. On a journey to the Continent he meets an older couple named Lucass, and finds his daughter-in-law, Pearl, attempting to leave her husband. Jack, his son, joins the train later in the journey. They experience a serious derailment which injures some, including Frith-Walter, and kills the driver. Arriving at their destination, the estranged couple go to separate hotels. Jack and his father join his mother at her hotel where eventually Jack takes the step that reconciles his wife to him. Frith-Walter finally relaxes with the loving supportiveness of his wife.

Frith-Walter believes the organization of society is desperately wrong, but labels even his own thoughts about the problem as futile and specious. The greatest problem with the book is that Frith-Walter's ponderings never become more than futile and specious. Of some value is the travelogue Frith-Walter provides in his musings: the sense of an almost isolated movement through country and towns, day and night, sunshine and snow, to the accompaniment of the noises of the train which seems to have an intention of its own removed from human aims. Trains were very much in the minds of all Britons just a few months before Bennett began to write the novel as the great general strike had been called in May. In that period Bennett was dining with Siegfried Sassoon whose timely poem *Morning Express* captures similar effects to Bennett's description of the environs of a terminal as the powerful locomotive glides in.[6]

Bennett's handling of the accident itself is well done. The reader experiences Frith-Walter's sensations as moment by moment the bashing of the derailed carriage breaks it apart. Well done also is the buildup of suspense from the first unexpected jarring stop of the train in the Kentish field to the accident itself in the mountains. Aiding the creation of suspense is the characterization of Mrs. Lucass as the temperamental, highly nervous, superstitious wife of the long-suffering, wealthy Tyneside manufacturer. She desperately wants to leave the train before a catastrophe overtakes it. Bennett seems to enjoy the creation of this narrow-eyed, faded, hysterical, sharp-tongued female who can still exert a charm and impose herself believably upon Frith-Walter, and who has kept the love of her old husband. She is the most vital creature in the book. The total is competent and readable without significance.

Imperial Palace

Imperial Palace has eighty-five speaking characters and is crammed with staggering detail. It is a monument to Bennett's fascination with organizations and systems. As readers have found, in spite of its seemingly dull subject—the operation of a *hotel de luxe*—in spite of its daunting 630-page length, the novel takes hold of one's imagination. Perhaps only Bennett could have felt drawn to such a subject; perhaps only he could turn his enthusiasm for a luxury hotel into almost a best seller during the Depression years.

That he had set himself a huge task, he was well aware. He wrote to Sir George Reeves-Smith, managing director of the Savoy group of hotels, that the material he had supplied Bennett "was enough for a dozen novels" and that he was having "the greatest difficulty in controlling it, and subduing it to the background of the tale proper."[7] He thrilled to the challenge and feared it might be beyond his powers. However, after its publication he was able to write to Harriet Cohen that, in the main, reviews were excellent.[8] He cited one critic particularly—Ivor Brown—who wrote in the *Observer* that Bennett "has achieved, not a mere technical triumph, but a triumph of technique."[9] That praise still stands.

It is impossible to give an adequate and brief synopsis of this complex compendium of hotel activities. The "tale proper" concerns Evelyn Orcham, the managing director of the Imperial Palace. He has achieved a point of perfection in the luxury and efficiency of the hotel that has given him world-renown. A widower, he has equally efficiently organized his personal life with the help of a valet and resides in the hotel. It is clear that he has no life apart from the hotel nor feels the need of more. However, with the appearance of the financier Sir Henry Savotte and his daughter Gracie, Evelyn's comfortable clockwork existence is disturbed on both the public and private levels. Gracie first pursues him, then runs away to Paris. Sir Henry also shakes Evelyn's complacency by suggesting he is only maintaining a rut at the hotel. He should ambitiously take up new challenges in a wider sphere Sir Henry would like to create by a merger of great hotels.

After Gracie's departure Evelyn discovers Violet Powler who has been employed as staff manager at the hotel laundry. Her calm self-possession and sense of humor impress him so that he transfers her to the hotel as a floor housekeeper. There she succeeds well and is recognized as the sister of a woman Sir Henry Savotte had hoped to marry following his divorce, only the young woman had died. When Savotte persuades Evelyn to agree to become managing director of a chain of hotels, his new duties carry him to Paris where Gracie seeks him again, seduces him, and quarrels with him. He returns to London where events make Violet more noticeable. The novel ends with Evelyn deciding to marry her.

Rounding out this tale in an almost incredible way are the multitudinous events within the hotel complex which includes thirty departments each with its own hierarchy of command. We are told that there are thirteen hundred employees in levels of the basement alone. We are given statistics of the artesian wells that give the hotel its own water supply and create its own hydroelectric power. We are taken through the boiler rooms, the laundry, the furniture makers, the kitchens and restaurants, the stock vaults, the accounts department, the variety of personnel offices, the housekeepers' and maids' domains, differing suites of rooms, up the halls, down the elevators, in and out of the great front entrance. We see the comings and goings of its clientele. We see its views through windows, its floodlighted dome against the night sky. All is presented in detail so minute that we are aware of the colored threads by which the laundry is sorted and the numbered tabs on carpets which permit through coded duplicate supplies the exact replacement of a soiled carpet within the hour. In almost every one of the areas mentioned Bennett gives the background of one or more of the key people and shapes events for them to give the sense of ongoing private lives having triumphs and failures within the routine of the hotel. Gradually Bennett makes the reader amazed at the mass, both human and material, requiring control and direction.

Out of this attitude, Bennett draws the degree of respect necessary to appreciate Evelyn Orcham's view of himself and to believe in his attraction for Gracie Savotte. Evelyn is not the lovable creation that Edwin Clayhanger is, nor is he the agonizing solitary Raingo. He is not a particularly likable character, nor does Bennett intend him to be. But he has shaped an ambition and acquired all that was necessary to the polished accomplishment of that ambition. He is undisputed autocrat of the Imperial Palace, but wields his powers with a diplomacy Bennett illustrates again and again. However, that he is prepared to be ruthless in discipline is also demonstrated. His power rests upon his ability to persuade all personnel to accept the mandate that justice for the individual is inseparable from justice to the institution. This code becomes the rock against which Gracie dashes herself and breaks her relationship with Evelyn. It is because Violet respects the code, but is able to bring Evelyn to accept a possible exception to every rule, that her relationship with him prospers.

Bennett shapes the "tale proper" to show Evelyn's wavering between two sets of values: the set represented by the hotel and Violet, and the set represented by Gracie. It is part of the ironies within the tale that Evelyn does not choose. He is chosen against by Gracie. To oppose the immense presentation of the hotel, with Violet treated as little more than the personification of the hotel—an asset—Bennett needed to produce a strong character indeed in Gracie Savotte. This he does without question. Gracie is the most powerful realization of the "new woman" in Bennett's fiction. She imposes herself upon the imagination from her entry to the hotel in chapter two.

To the uninterested gaze of the meat-buyer awaiting Evelyn in the lobby for a visit to the famous Smithfield Market, Gracie with her expensive dashing clothes and vivacious manner is a "prancing hussy." To Evelyn, her forthright, unusual statements, her beauty and high fashion, make her "irresistible." She projects the sense of being intelligent and intensely alive. Her initial effect on Evelyn reminds one of Hilda's effect on Edwin—she astonishes him into being uncharacteristically forthright himself. After she asks him to take her to the meat market, and while expertly driving him there, she suddenly asks: "What brought *you* into the hotel business?" He replied as suddenly: "The same thing that brought you to motoring. Instinct."[10]

This statement becomes more significant as their relationship develops. Her instinct is to speak and act out of the totality of what she feels at the moment. Her conversation is never social chatter. Before the drive ends at the market, she tells Evelyn what she admires in him is that he doesn't act the role of the big man the way her father and others do. He is amazed at her insight. When she smoothly parks her car and arranges with a policeman to watch it for her, Bennett ends the chapter: "Evelyn, accustomed to take charge of all interviews, parleys, and pow-wows, had to be a silent spectator" (19). The essence of their attraction for each other and one factor in their separation appears here. Gracie believes that what the instincts suggest is right, that all pretense must be cast aside, that a woman and a man must come together in equality for real love to exist. She finds this man attractive and from his behavior and statements she begins to believe he may be wholly the man she can love. As they leave the meat market Bennett writes: "She wanted ardently to be a man among men; she felt that she was capable of being a man among men. . . . She persuaded herself that he knew all her thoughts" (27).

Evelyn might be prepared to agree that instincts should be followed, but his entire past and present have involved him in the preservation of facades, and he cannot contemplate a male-female relationship where the male is not the undisputed master. For a time Gracie's astonishing novelty sweeps Evelyn along. Bennett shapes few encounters for the pair. But each encounter seems to Evelyn to leap years of getting acquainted and propels him to undreamed-of intimacy. He early recognizes and consciously tries to change his bias— "a bit too much of the Oriental attitude" (66), "he suffered from masculine timidity and conventionality" (68). It is Gracie who makes all the moves. She arranges that she and her father dine with him in the hotel restaurant where they watch a particularly sensuous dance team and where she tricks Evelyn into dancing with her so closely that he is very conscious of her body. She asks to see the kitchens. They tour the area which causes her to say desperately that she *must* work and she mentions having started her writing. Then she plans a small party which Evelyn refuses to attend. She faces him with the fact that he is holding her off and when he blandly continues to refuse, she leaves in a fury. Next morning she goes to Paris.

She returns to London at New Year's Eve to see about the publication of her book *Sensations and Ideas* and brings with her her unmarried, pregnant maid Tessa who takes an attack in the night. Evelyn, hearing that Gracie is in the hotel and that there has been a miscarriage, goes to the suite to inquire. Violet Powler calmly tells him all is under control and the maid's baby is still safe. Gracie's attitude toward the event further amazes him, but it serves to heal the breach between them.

Bennett shapes ten chapters primarily of dialogue to develop Evelyn's and Gracie's affair from renewal to her avowal, her disappointment, and her sending him off. It is the most vivid dialogue in Bennett's fiction. Gracie's intelligent grasp of the whole situation is dramatically realized and must have struck sensitive contemporary readers as having as much truth, point, and power as some of D. H. Lawrence's writing. The floundering Evelyn's reactions are equally well done.

Bennett does not create anything like the vital presence of Gracie in Violet Powler. We see her in word and deed prove to be the fairly undemanding wife that Evelyn believes he is glad to settle for. Bennett does not make her a cipher, but she is colorless compared to Gracie. Nevertheless, she can challenge Evelyn and impose her will at times. Her effect throughout the levels of the hotel establishes her worth. Her quiet joy in her love of Evelyn is suggested. There is not the heady passion in Evelyn's feeling for her that marked his simplest contact with Gracie, but Bennett indicates that Evelyn's basic instincts in love could not raise him to the level on which Gracie's instincts normally functioned. He chooses to ally himself with a woman whose instincts mirror his own. There is nothing to suggest that there is any loss for him in the conclusion. On the contrary, there is a sense of his having triumphed on his level.

Venus Rising From the Sea and *Dream of Destiny*

Venus Rising From the Sea was dashed off in April and May of 1929. It is short—a little over a hundred pages—and perfunctory. It features the struggle of Etta Wickhamsted, an actress who had become an overnight success in a role she had only been hired to understudy. Because the play has a long run, she is typecast as a vamp and finds it impossible later to secure equivalent roles. After some years she drops out of sight, but continues to haunt theatrical agencies hoping her luck will change.

She shares a poor bed-sitter with her cousin. Where Etta is slim, ladylike, self-possessed, and quiet, Agatha Stockney, nicknamed Stocky, is buxom, unladylike, loud, and arrogant. By chance, Etta, returning from her latest disappointment at an agency, saves a baby who is about to step in front of an approaching car. The driver is exceedingly grateful, asks her name and address, and plans to send her flowers. He proves to be Maurice Leverton, a famous playwright, who pursues his interest in Etta. Stocky's jealousy is aroused and she leaves their shared accommodations, not before securing a bit-part from Leverton. Etta has not been offered a role, but is asked to read the unfinished script of Leverton's latest effort as he has come to respect her critical views. Their conferences over the script lead to Leverton's declaration of love, her return to the stage for a star role in the finished play, and at the end of the run, her engagement to him.

Bennett barely referred to financial arrangements concerning this book in his Journal. It is perhaps the least noticeable of his potboilers. The only interest one can see lies in the indications of Bennett's knowledge of the details of the poverty-stricken arrangement of these girls for existing in their bed-sitter. It reminds one again of Bennett's amazing absorption of details of levels of living.

In *Dream of Destiny*, however, there are suggestions of more substance. In September, 1930, in a letter to Eric Pinker, Bennett wrote:

I am already very keen on my next novel, and the scheme of it is complete. I shall begin it in December and it will be finished—I think—about May. It is based on the plot of the story 'The Dream' which you sold to some newspaper in Chicago. If I had seen the possibilities of that plot earlier I should never have squandered it on a short story.[11]

Bennett began the novel in November. He did not live until May. He completed only one fifth of his intention of the novel, then succumbed to typhoid fever.

In the same letter to Pinker he referred to another short story that had been turned into the novel *The Glimpse*. There is another link between these tales in that *Dream of Destiny* also focuses upon a parapsychological phenomenon. In this case, the central figure Roland Smith, upon going to a housewarming for his cousin, meets there the attractive Phoebe Friar, an actress recently returned from New York. He is certain he has met her before and in that garden. He knows this is his first visit to the garden and she insists that they've never met before. As she talks, he remembers a powerful dream of two nights before. More and more of it returns from his subconscious. He had loved, married, and watched this woman die in childbirth. His instincts are to run from her.

Bennett shapes Phoebe to have something of the magnetism and forthrightness of Gracie Savotte. He again makes the female the pursuer in that Phoebe seeks occasions to be with Roland Smith. Roland responds to Phoebe, captivated by her in every way, but fights his instincts because he feels himself to be her potential murderer. What Bennett would have developed from this cannot be speculated. The novel ends at a point where, exhausted by a successful opening of a new play in which she is the acclaimed star, confused and disturbed by Roland's reaction to her, Phoebe has had a nervous breakdown in which her violence toward Roland decides her doctor that under no circumstances must he see her again for a period of time.

Within the chapters completed Bennett, making Roland Smith a designer and manager of a block of cheap flats, indulges again in his

fascination with organizations and efficiency in living. The perception that efficiency in living may preclude value in life begins to
trouble Roland Smith at the point where the novel ends.

Bennett's last years exhibit as much dynamism as any group of
years in his life. They show him attempting feats he had never
before approached. The psychological study of *Lord Raingo*, the
sustained effort of *Imperial Palace*, the inclusion in the latter of
deftly handled explicit sex, all indicate that the author was not a
burned-out old man, that, in fact, his greatest work may have been
to come. His untimely death is therefore doubly unfortunate.

Chapter Eight
Other Writings

Bennett gave first place to his novels. However, he brought a zest to the writing of short stories, plays, reviews, reminiscences, practical advice, and produced such quantities of each type, that no assessment of the author can be complete without some reference to this other body of his work. Variety and a characteristic vigor distinguish most of the mass.

The Short Stories

As mentioned earlier, Bennett received from *The Yellow Book* his first critical recognition with the publication in 1895 of his short story "The Letter Home." This reappears as the last in a group of thirteen stories entitled *Tales of the Five Towns* (1905).[1] Six other volumes of short stories followed over the years: *The Loot of Cities* (eight tales, 1905), *The Grim Smile of the Five Towns* (thirteen tales, 1907), *The Matador of the Five Towns* (seventeen tales, 1912), *Elsie and the Child* (thirteen tales, 1924), *The Woman Who Stole Everything* (thirteen tales, 1927), and *The Night Visitor and Other Stories* (seventeen tales, 1931). The successive volumes do not show a progression in Bennett's use of the genre. Primarily, the stories feature expansions of anecdotes of Five Towns "cards" or develop experiences of types constantly present to Bennett's imagination such as the quixotic millionaire, the arrogant artist, the managing wife, the temperamental thoroughbred, the stoical laborer. Much of the action involves either domestic difficulties or extravagant, improbable intrigue and mystery. However, some of the volumes include well-wrought and distinguished tales.

In Bennett's first volume, besides "The Letter Home," there is the affecting tale of "Tiddy-fol-lol" and the notable "His Worship the Goosedriver," one of Bennett's favorites. The last-mentioned tale opens the volume with the account of Josiah Curtenty, jolly Deputy Mayor of Bursley, who, piqued by a goosedriver's comment that there is no business in Bursley, buys all his unsold geese.

Then, nettled by his friend's mocking statements, he takes the goosedriver's staff and prepares to drive the geese to his home. As Bennett develops the consequences of Curtenty's precipitation, he accurately captures the humor and the difficulty of the walk home, the inimical attitude of Curtenty's wife and the citizenry of Bursley, and ends the tale with a face-saving feast for Curtenty engineered by his wife and friend. The whimsy of the tale is capably caught.

In "Tiddy-fol-lol," Bennett depicts the affecting story of a taciturn old man's striking his handicapped grandson for taunting him with others in the street. The boy, afflicted with a hearing impairment, stammering, and a clouded intellect, lies in a coma for a day. All fear he will die; but his recovery with removal of his earlier ailments seems so miraculous to his grandfather, that the old man becomes reconciled to the boy's mother from whom he had been estranged after her poor marriage. The pathos in this Five Towns fairy tale is better handled in "The Letter Home," the concluding story of the volume. This tale depicts a young man who had disappointed his family, squandered his resources, and come to die as a vagrant in a hospital ward. His last effort is expended in writing a letter to his mother expressing his sorrow. Another friendly vagrant offers to post the letter. Later, when wishing to light a pipe, the tramp pulls the crumpled paper from his pocket and sets fire to it. The sombre representation of waste and futility is quite artistically achieved. The coherent power in the concise narrative vindicates its early publication in *The Yellow Book*.

In the second volume, *The Loot of Cities*, Bennett organizes into chapters separate adventures featuring the same two characters, Cecil Thorold, eccentric millionaire, and Eve Fincastle, journalist, who believes Thorold to be an unprincipled wretch. Thorold delights in uncovering thieves and frauds, always to his own financial gain. Bennett concocts something of the whimsical intrigue and mystery of *The Grand Babylon Hotel*, but sets the scenes on the Gold Coast, in Algiers, in the Sahara desert. The combinations of character, situation, and scene are capably constructed. The remaining stories in the volume mainly feature strange poisonings, burglaries, anarchist's assassinations.

The Grim Smile of the Five Towns, Bennett's third volume, includes his best short story. "The Death of Simon Fuge" is a well-wrought, subtle revelation of character. It is set within a collection of tales all capturing aspects of Five Towns people wryly admired by Bennett. The narrator, a British Museum expert on pottery, approaches the Midlands for the first time, having met the Bursley artist Fuge in London years before, and having just read of his death in a select newspaper on the train. Slowly, but with sure strokes, Bennett suggests the interests of the controlled, sensitive aesthete who appreciated Fuge's art and who had formed a fascination for the liberated artist, relishing particularly Fuge's lack of reticence in talking of himself. Vividly remembering Fuge's brilliant personality and his graphic account of a night spent in a boat on Ilam Lake with two beautiful Bursley sisters, Loring is titillated again with "the delicious possibility of ineffable indiscretions"[2] on the part of the artist and curious to enter the region of Fuge's birth.

In choosing this narrator, Bennett cleverly could register the shock of the intelligent, sensitive outsider's first experiences of the Black Country, and delineate believably Loring's attempts to reconcile the fact that the grimy industrial region could produce an artist of the stature of Fuge, while being forced to respond to the vigor of residents who cannot be dismissed as crude provincials lacking culture. At Knype station he is surrounded with "a pushing, exclamatory, ill-dressed, determined crowd" (212). All he saw around him "was a violent negation of Simon Fuge" (213). Bennett aptly captures the biases of this cloistered, studious man upon meeting his host, Robert Brindley, a hearty architect dressed like a country squire.

In Brindley's company Loring sees the scale of ugliness in the singular scenery of the Five Towns as so vast that it is sublime. Assuming that Brindley seldom if ever read the *Gazette*, he ventures to question Brindley about it, only to have him put the paper down for "rotten" musical criticism. Upon pulling himself together, he decides Brindley "was a man; he was a very tonic dose" (219). His experiences in Brindley's home with good food, good music, good books, unceremonious friendliness, lead him to indulge himself to the point of exclaiming "Never before or since have I been such a buck" (236). Loring's experiences end with his meeting the two sisters with whom Fuge had rowed on the lake. One is a superior barmaid, the other the contented wife of Brindley's friend. Loring strains to preserve his notion of Fuge's dalliance with these women, but can find no corroboration of illicit romance in the facts the Five Towns' people offer him. He leaves the area with an appreciation of its genuine hospitality, its unique combination of the brusque and the sensitive in its people. Bennett's mastery of the material is evident in the ease with which humor, movement, conversations, descriptions, all cohere, with no false note struck, to give the reader a sense of the honesty and insight in characterization and milieu.

The remaining volumes include no equally distinguished work. In *The Matador of the Five Towns*, the Loring of "Simon Fuge" narrates in a tale with the same title a subsequent visit to the Five Towns, but he is too much the author's tool as observer of life in the Potteries. The other tales mainly emphasize the fears, the illusions, the maneuverings of both sexes in various stages of marriage, or feature Five Towns' "cards" and curmudgeons gaining their own ways, or getting humorously caught by their own tricks. Bennett's use of the form as a source of relaxation causes the successive volumes to be mainly superficial entertainments.

The Plays

From his earliest years in London Bennett showed a fascination for the theater. His first published effort was a collection of three one-act plays for the drawing-room—a natural choice for the enthusiastic organizer of artistic evenings at the Marriotts'. Entitled *Polite Farces for the Drawing Room* (n.d.[1899]), it includes *The Stepmother*, *A Good Woman*, and *A Question of Sex*. The first involves a popular self-important lady novelist, her stepson, a doctor, and her witty secretary. The dialogue has considerable sophistication and humor with the secretary scoring most points on the foibles of the novelist. She maneuvers situations so that the novelist thankfully accepts the love of the doctor, while she can then safely marry the stepson. It is quite amusing.

The second play, *A Good Woman*, was used as a curtain raiser in later years. It has more absurd action with the triangle of Rosamund Fife, James Brett, and Gerald O'Mara. Rosamund and James are about to go to the Registry Office to marry when Gerald appears to claim her promise to marry him made four years before as he was about to go to Cyprus. The heights of the ridiculous are reached as Rose first decides she will marry Gerald, then, after the men have almost had a shooting match, she decides to marry James with Gerald agreeing to act as witness. The dialogue has much superficial wit.

In the third play, *A Question of Sex*, George Gower attempts to gain an inheritance from his bachelor uncle by pretending the child newly born to him is a boy. He hasn't had time to acquaint his wife, his sister, or his sister-in-law with the pretense, so much comedy of situation develops when the uncle comes to pay his respects. The competency in humor achieved in the first two farces is maintained here. Bennett's next dramatic effort was much more substantial.

After moving to Paris to live, he made a special trip back to England in 1909 to see *What the Public Wants* produced on the West End stage. It first opened at the Aldwych and was successful enough to be put on again at the Royalty where it ran for a month and gained Max Beerbohm's commendation. The play has much more substance than the early farces in that Bennett develops a believable portrait of a rather crass tycoon of the popular press who expects to end his career in the House of Lords. As the play proceeds, much of newspaper ethics and intellectual aesthetics is examined. The various attitudes are given interesting form in the male-female situations chosen.

In the same year *Cupid and Commonsense* was staged in Glasgow. It is a travesty on *Anna of the Five Towns*, making Alice a much less subtly complex Anna; making Emily a pert, managing girl far removed from the timid, sensitive Agnes; allowing Willie Beach to become a coarsened successful businessman with a crass American wife instead of the pathetic suicide Willie Price; and having Alice (Anna) give big receptions as wife of the Mayor at the end. Nothing about the play would particularly recommend it.

The Honeymoon, also written in the same year, was first accepted for the Haymarket Theatre in 1910, but was not produced there. It was sold in 1911 to Marie Tempest who performed the lead role of Flora Lloyd at the Royalty for the play's run of four months. The simple plot turns on a bridal couple arguing before the honeymoon over the groom's wish to postpone it while he enters a flying competition. Their interesting unconventional argument culminates in Flora's asking Cedric if he thinks she should yield to the airplane. He concedes her point, but his concession, because it is a concession, leaves her feeling despair. The act ends with the news of their sham marriage ceremony. For the next two acts Bennett develops the conflict between Flora and her prospective mother-in-law, a famous popular novelist whose writings and attitudes Flora obviously disdains, and Cedric's attempts to reinstate himself in Flora's affections in spite of his mother's lack of enthusiasm for it. Throughout the play there is clever dialogue, quick changes of mood and situation, effectively accomplished with a sophistication that drew Marie Tempest's admiration and would entertain audiences today.

Bennett next collaborated with Edward Knoblock upon *Milestones*, his most successful play. The idea and construction dramatizing family tensions over generations was Knoblock's, but ninety-eight percent of the dialogue Bennett claimed.[3] The play with a distinguished cast opened at the Royalty in 1912, won excellent reviews, and ran for a year. It gave audiences the pleasure of watching excellent performers age before their eyes, while following the consequences over three generations of attitudes common to the viewers.

Of the first generation, John Rhead and his sister Gertrude are both young progressives while Samuel Sibley, John's partner in shipbuilding, is conservative. His sister Rose is obedient. When John wants to build iron ships instead of wooden ones, Samuel Sibley refuses to consider it. John breaks the partnership and Gertrude breaks her engagement to Samuel. Twenty-five years later John has become the conservative, expecting his daughter Emily to marry into the aristocracy as he wishes. She is in love with a young engineer, but she follows her father's wishes much to her Aunt Gertrude's disgust. Twenty-five years pass again, and Emily tries to impose her wishes on her daughter Muriel, but the young girl, supported by her grandmother Rose and her Great-aunt Gertrude, follows her heart and marries where she pleases. This content is well wrought in dialogue to give the principal performers scope for effective presentations. Its revival in 1929 by Dorothy Cheston Bennett brought reviews acclaiming it again.

The Great Adventure of 1913 was also an immediate success. It was a dramatized version of *Buried Alive* directed by Harley Granville Barker at the Kingsway. It ran for nine months with critics and public lauding Wish Wynne in the role of the pathologically shy artist's wife. The novel adapted well to the stage, and when it too gained another respectable run in 1924, it was greeted by critics as a happy revival. The year of *The Great Adventure* saw Bennett's completion of a play he had begun planning in 1909. It was never performed. The play *Don Juan de Marana* does not come to life at any point. Don Juan's succession of affairs provides a series of haughty women, willing or unwilling victims of his passions, who all go to their deaths, until on a dare, Juan tries to seduce a nun, experiences a vision from which he survives with her help, and finally joins a monastery. Attempts to capture the aristocratic milieu of medieval Spain are partially successful, but none of the characters in the action has reality. In the preface to a privately printed edition of the play in 1923 Bennett defends his choice of the Spanish lover. He says: "In drama, as in some other forms of literature, the theme is the most important thing. . . . But for me the point is that my Don Juan *has* an ideal. He is not a sensualist; he is an idealist. He is passionately hungry for perfection; and with him the end justifies the means."[4] Bennett failed to animate the theory.

A third novel dramatization was made in 1916 when Bennett contracted to rewrite *Sacred and Profane Love* for the actress Doris Keane. She did not like the version so it did not reach the stage until 1919. It ran first in Liverpool, then at the Aldwych in London for over a hundred performances. The play includes more characters than the novel, omits all of the ironic overtones, and changes the ending to have Diaz recognize his debt to Carlotta. She does not die but expects happiness with Diaz to continue. It is reasonable theatrical fare, but totally undistinguished.

In 1918 Bennett wrote *The Title—A Comedy in Three Acts*. It features the Culver family of four and Tranto, an editor and relative of earls, baronets, and other press lords. Tranto's paper *The Echo* has just published an anti-title article by their correspondent Samuel Straight, who secretly is Hildegarde Culver. Some of Tranto's relatives think he is Sam Straight and find the writings against titles and hereditary holdings upsetting. Mr. Culver, obviously disturbed, has been offered a title in the new Honors list. He knows his daughter is Sam Straight and plans to refuse the title. Mrs. Culver is prepared to disrupt their marriage over this. After a man actually bearing the name of Sam Straight tries to pass himself off to the family as the writer, and after the family learns that the government means to honor Sam Straight if Culver refuses the knighthood, all is resolved with Culver accepting the title. The play provides a considerable number of amusing moments and makes the most of the noteworthy points about the granting of titles. Bennett himself a few years later was offered and refused a knighthood.

Following the war, Bennett not only continued to produce plays but became very much involved in supporting theatrical productions, most notably those of the Lyric Theatre, Hammersmith. His membership in the Board and his financial backing made it possible for the Lyric to produce five plays in a period practically devoted to frivolous entertainments. In this period Lillah Macarthy renewed her pressure on Bennett to write a play for her. He responded with the exotic play *Judith*. The biblical account of the Hebrew Judith saving Judea by seducing and killing Holofernes, the leader of the marauding troops of Nebuchadnezzar, gave plenty of scope for gorgeous pageantry, and provocative scenes for Lillah. But the weight of the historical presentation limits the characters, slows the action, and requires period dialogue that is not maintained. However, Lillah Macarthy liked it, its first audiences in Eastbourne liked it, but its opening at the Kingsway in London was generally given bad reviews. When one considers that Bennett got it all together in less than a month, the wonder is that he could imaginatively grasp the setting and period as well as he did. It is interesting to read, but clearly not the script for lively action on stage.

Bennett's next three plays, *The Love Match*, *Body and Soul*, and *The Bright Island*, were all written in 1922. The first two have a common element in that a female is taught a lesson in her relationship with a male. In the first, a millionaire takes his lover away from her husband, marries her, finds her extravagant, autocratic with servants, and planning to manage his life for him. He pretends to a bankruptcy and lets her learn to economize in poor accommodations. Discovering it is a trick, she, with the help of her worldly wise sister, is reconciled to her husband and restored to gracious living. Bennett has opportunity for much clever repartee between husband and wife typical of a number of his earlier plays. In *Body and Soul* there is a more farcical central conflict in that a wealthy society girl, interested in spiritualism, and planning to marry an ordinary northern businessman, decides to let her favorite spiritualist transform her newly hired secretary into herself by hypnotism while she pretends to be the secretary for awhile. The secretary Blanche, a shrewd northern girl, decides to play up to the plot unknown to her employer. She takes over the lady's role with a vengeance, delights in acting affectionate to her employer's fiancé, and, in a public speech to a northern community, disarms the laborers with her socialist statements and gives largesse from her employer's funds. Lady Mab, considering herself ruined and chastened, breaks her engagement, and through a rich uncle secures a job lecturing in America. It is a slight comedy, but Bennett expected it to run well. However, even with Viola Tree as Lady Mab, the play ran for less than a month. The third play is another strange departure in form for Bennett, not to ancient biblical times, but to a fantasy island with commedia dell'arte characters side by side with modern British types. Rights of women, causes of laborer's strikes, attitudes of husbands and wives, difficulty of dictatorships, all receive farcical treatment in this absurd amalgam. But it provides humorous reading.

Another play written in 1922, but not performed until 1924, is *London Life* written in collaboration with Edward Knoblock. No doubt Bennett hoped to repeat their success of *Milestones.* The play has a large cast, many changes of scene, and a complicated plot of the political maneuverings of a paper baron, a Bursley lawyer, and a titled aristocrat. All the familiars of the London social scene are there, but in none of the characters is there an achieved personality. The accuracy of much of the political action gathered from Bennett's friendship with Lord Beaverbrook has some interest, but that does not save the play.

In 1925 Bennett's dramatized version of his novel *Mr. Prohack* went on stage at the Court Theatre. It launched the successful career of Charles Laughton as Prohack and brought Dorothy Cheston back to the stage in the role of Lady Massulam. The play proved to be a popular success, but its longer run was cut short by the need to move to a new theater and the loss of Laughton in the attempted transfer. The amusing Prohack of the novel is given an abundance of occasions to identify and comically mock many human foibles. Laughton made the most of all the script's opportunities to raise hilarious laughter. Also in this year the only production of *Flora* took place in Manchester. It was written in March. Bennett felt the play had "holding power"[5] when he went to view a performance. The drama features Flora's desire for satisfying work now that her daughter is grown up. Her hypochon-

driacal husband refuses to allow her need. Flora leaves him, takes
up managing a night club, is about to begin an affair with its owner,
when her husband visits the club to inform her that their daughter
wants to live with her lover and does not plan to marry. This
eventually brings both parents together although Flora finally, and
in secret, encourages her daughter to go with her love. The play is
not distinguished; but it interested Mrs. Patrick Campbell, although she failed to achieve a London production for it.

Bennett ended his dramatic career as he began it with one-act
plays. He copyrighted two short plays in 1928 which are to be
found in Samuel French's collections of one-act plays for Stage and
Study.[6] *The Snake Charmer* is a melodrama reminiscent of Bennett's early serials. The dark, lovely, Carman-like Geralda, dressed
in a snake-ornamented dress, leads Tomlinson, elegant, ruined
scoundrel, into her Parisian apartment. Ten years before, when she
was only seventeen, he had seduced her into a marriage that was
six months of hell before they parted. Now she plans her revenge.
After she has humiliated him into a rage, he is about to shoot her
when the lights go out and they are shocked by smoke and a red
glare. He goes mad and jumps out the window. She faints and is
rescued by her present lover. *The Ides of March* written with Fred
Alcock is less lurid, but also melodramatic. A knighted physician is
visited by a veiled patient proving to be his former fiancée who had
married his brother instead. That brother had accepted exile for a
thieving scandal which he believed was the physician's act. His wife
comes now to her famous brother-in-law hoping he will help her
afflicted young son. After angry words which reveal all the past
truths, the physician, admiring her loyalty to his dead brother,
admits his guilt and agrees to treat her son's rare disease. In both
plays Bennett's dialogue engenders emotional power. The first has
the most theatrical dialogue and the characters never come to life;
the second has stilted dialogue in places, but has much more
realistic and believable characters in spite of the unbelievable plot.

Finally, although not a play, the film-story *Piccadilly* will be
considered here. A number of Bennett's novels were filmed, *The
City of Pleasure, The Card, The Old Wives' Tale*, but this was the first
original script he was asked to do. The film was first shown in
1929. The editor's note of a 1930s edition of the film-story claims
it was one of the most remarkable films recently produced and

drew a group of well-known stars for the cast. Photographs included in the 1975[7] edition of the story of the film indicate that it would be visually dazzling. Its plot had sufficient mystery and thrills to interest the young director Alfred Hitchcock. Briefly, the action centers on a sophisticated nightclub owner who becomes passionately involved with a young enigmatic Chinese dancer. He abandons his long-standing relationship with his aging star dancer as patronage of his club begins to decline. Seeing the young Chinese girl dance in his kitchen, he tries her exoticism on his clientele and has a booming success. Mesmerized by the girl, he eventually makes love to her in the Chinatown of London's East End. At the height of her power over him, she is mysteriously murdered. He is implicated, but after an inquest a young Chinese man is found guilty. The nightclub owner returns to his faithful former lover. Bennett could exult that his film *Piccadilly* was a great success at the Carlton.[8] However, he felt that its direction had failed to convey much of his comedy and that the end of the film was not properly rounded off.[9]

In retrospect, Bennett's activities in theatrical writing for stage and film emphasize his enthusiasm for extending himself into all literary forms in prose. Again, the quantity is remarkable. It is obvious that he did not view his plays as much more than timely entertainments which could air important ideas, but which did not explore them with any profundity. They were usually comic romps of one kind or another.

Criticism and Other Miscellaneous Writing

The bulk of Bennett's writing in this category is so large that only a cursory glance at some of the interesting elements is possible here. From 1908 to 1911 Bennett produced a series of weekly articles on fiction and the fiction-reading public for *The New Age* entitled "Books and Persons" under the pseudonym Jacob Tonson. A selection of about one third of these articles was published in book form in 1917 as *Books and Persons Being Comments on a Past Epoch 1908–1911*. A similar series was begun in 1926 when Beaverbrook bought the *Evening Standard* and asked Bennett to resume his role of critic with a series of articles again to be headed "Books and Persons."[10] From 1926 to his death Bennett fulfilled the role.

Both series gave the author eminence as the most powerful and important reviewer of books in England. With independence from all cliques and coteries, in a style succinct, thoughtful, provocative, he achieved a rapport with his readers from all levels of society which enabled him to move their perspectives into the modern age. He is credited with being the first to bring the genius of Chekov to recognition in England; his praise of Dostoevski with a call to Heinemann for an English edition had the sensational effect of bringing within six weeks Heinemann's announcement of a proposed first English edition. His early appreciations of Joyce, Woolf, Lawrence brought wider recognition to them. His influence cannot be overestimated. Naturally, all of his judgments were not equally valuable in that he had his enthusiasms and limitations. However, he never confused his standards; he always distinguished the literary artist from the popular writer as he had always made this clear distinction in his own works.

A sampling of his judgments will show how he could be so attractive and influential: of Conrad's *Lord Jim*—"one of the most noble examples of fine composition in modern literature"; of Thomas Hardy—"a seer of beauty"; of Chekov—"we have no writer, and we have never had one, nor has France, who could mold the material of life, without distorting it, into such complex forms to such an end of beauty. Read these books, and you will genuinely know something about Russia; you will be drenched in the vast melancholy, savage and wistful, of Russian life; and you will have seen beauty."

His negatives are to the point: of Mrs. Humphrey Ward's heroines—"harrowing dolls," of Anatole France's latest writings—"spiritual anaemia," of Henry James—"in the fastidiousness of his taste he rather repudiated life." Of some obvious young talents he held typical reservations. Having picked Virginia Woolf's *To the Lighthouse* as the "most original" of a group of new novels he'd read, and after calling it "the best book of hers I know," he says "Mrs. Ramsay almost amounts to a complete person," and the scheme of the book is "wilful," yet "there are some pleasing records of interesting sensations outside the range of the ordinary novelist." In a later article he could honestly say he feels sure in the light of history "that our best new authors will escape my questioning gaze. . . . or, chancing to see them, I shall fail to recognize them for what they are." The remarkable fact for his readers, then and now, is how wide a field he surveyed—English, French, Russian, German, American writers—and how accurate so many of his identifications of talent proved to be.

Throughout his life after coming to London Bennett noted in some form all he did and saw and thought about. His published *Journals* attest remarkably to this daily habit. Periodically, he would put together compilations of these writings, such as *Paris Nights and Other Impressions of People and Places* (1913). Many of the descriptions of people, places, and events are quite effective. But the mass included seems an indulgence. *Things That Have Interested Me* (1921) is another collection, but includes some literary criticism. Bennett had a second series published under this title in 1923 and a third series in 1926. They are reproductions of short pieces privately published in 1906, 1907, and 1908 under the title *Things That Have Interested Me.* He said of the series: "These impressions deal with both life and the arts . . . They are certainly as interesting as *Books and Persons.* But in the main, they are not popular, nor intended so to be; they are my lark."[11]

In the first volume he imaginatively captures place in describing a performance of *Die Meistersinger* at Covent Garden; he describes the "voluptuous" onset and dissipation of fatigue; he gives a vignette of an oldish woman in a hotel dining room fussing over a breakfast menu which disturbs Bennett until her husband comes. Bennett is mollified to discover that she was anxious over her husband's breakfast and he observes their contented relationship with pleasure. In the second volume, in the article "Sex-Rivalry," Bennett shows his understanding of women and women's position that impressed female readers of his day. Indeed, statements that women in the home need to have their services recognized and remunerated would impress female readers today. The same article would annoy strong feminists, however, because Bennett postulates that one duty of a wife is "consciously to exercise charm." Included in this series is his review praising parts of Joyce's *Ulysses* as "unsurpassed." In the third series he writes of his feelings upon first entering the Ministry of Information in 1919, which were echoed in his novel *Lord Raingo*; he writes of clothes and the man, of a murderer's confession, of benevolence, life's greatest satisfaction. In this volume, also, he gives a good estimate of Marcel Proust. A similar volume, although not of this series, is *The Savour of Life* (1928).

Sometimes, after Bennett had traveled, he published volumes of his journeys. These were illustrated by his own water-color sketches, charcoal and pencil drawings, many of considerable competence. An early volume, not published until 1967, is the *Florentine Journal* of 1910. Sacheverell Sitwell attests in the Preface to Bennett's accurate capturing of place in it. *From the Log of the Velsa* (1920) and *Mediterranean Scenes* (1928) combine pieces of documentary presentation with more imaginative impressions of scene. Bennett's estimate of method for this kind of literature was cited in an article of 1930 where he said: "Now a book of impressions of travel can be written in at least two ways: either as a *book*, with set chapters carefully constructed, or as a succession of vignettes each cursive, complete, rapid. . . . I prefer the latter."[12] The best of these vignettes is not in the volumes listed above, however, but is included as the last entry entitled "Unknown Southern France" in *Things That Have Interested Me. Second Series* (1923). There his descriptions bear comparison with Robert Louis Stevenson's beguiling *Travels with a Donkey*. Although he preferred writing the vignettes, the journey he shaped as a book, entitled *Those United States* (1912), includes a fascinating description of the *Lusitania* in transit, and is remarkably interesting throughout.

Of the remaining writings, his "pocket philosophies," and his "How To" books, have at times brought sneering comments. Nevertheless, Bennett has a refreshing way of treating the platitudes of *Friendship and Happiness* (1911); his *Mental Efficiency* (1920) and *How to Live on 24 Hours a Day* (1908) are sensible. His *How To Become An Author* (1903) and *Literary Taste* (1909) are very well done indeed. They are readable, informative, and practical. His early tongue-in-cheek, anonymous account, *The Truth About an Author*, is amusing to read in conjunction with these practical guides. He delighted in tearing down veils of mystery raised around artistic activity. As he says in his preface to the 1914 edition of the work, "I took a malicious and frigid pleasure, as I always do, in setting down facts which are opposed to accepted sentimental falsities; and certainly I did not spare myself."[13] One remembers that Bennett had once said he would like his epitaph to be "He strove to destroy illusions."

There are those who have wished that Bennett had confined himself to writing novels. Given his temperament and principles, that would have been impossible for him. With the delight he obviously found in so much of the work, it is unsympathetic to wish he had not done it. In each category there is at least one or two of the works worth survival.

Chapter Nine
Conclusion

Arnold Bennett's best novels will never appeal to the reader who demands other than what Bennett's concept of the novel allowed him to produce. His opinion that a strictly limited prose was best suited to his presentation of very limited lives leaves him open to the distaste of readers who find immediate stimulation in Conrad's colorful prose, high adventure, and probings of unusual minds. Those readers who enjoy the delicate tracing of the obscure in the relationships of Henry James's characters, or in those of Virginia Woolf, will be offended at the matter-of-factness of Bennett's assumptions. Those readers who wish to exercise their ingenuity in following the convolutions of James Joyce will find Bennett's "abiding by the envelope of facts" deadly dull.

However, there can no longer be doubt that Arnold Bennett has produced some of the finest novels in the early twentieth century. From the mass of his fiction one can cite eight novels of outstanding art. When one rids oneself of the literary clichés provided by Henry James, Virginia Woolf, Ezra Pound, and critics who cannot countenance his production of "fantasias," "frolics," and "pocket philosophies," one can find much evidence in print of his extraordinary sensitivity to the concerns of his fellow artists, and of his equally extraordinary zeal in following his own insights.

One aspect of his work perhaps needs review here. Some sensitive readers leave Bennett's serious works with a consciousness of grayness and profound gloom exhibited in them. This study cannot substantiate that perception. With the microscope the dull ditch-water becomes a vibrant aquatic world. In Bennett's meticulous presentation of the ordinary, the scale has to be recognized. Not to perceive, or not to accept, his scale is to move toward sentimentalism in interpreting his results.

All of his figures recognize scope for choice and achievement in their lives. Particularly is this true of his frolics where easy material success is outrageously flaunted as the basis for happiness. But it is in the serious novels that his delicate perception of positives in the face of all negatives gains artistic expression. As this study has shown, Richard Larch in *A Man From the North* has a successful career and can become satisfied when false dreams are cast aside. Anna, in *Anna of the Five Towns*, though she may remain unawakened to passionate love, will not be desolate in her marriage. Her husband loves her and her marriage will conform to the only expectations she can have shaped for it. Sophia's tragedy in *The Old Wives' Tale* is countered by Constance's sense of the happiness of her life. Edwin and Hilda in the *Clayhanger* trilogy win their way through to a marriage that promises pleasurable excitement to the end. Some forget their contented appearance in old age in *The Roll Call*. Violet and Henry in *Riceyman Steps* know a heroic passion in spite of his obsession, and Elsie is a powerfully positive presence. Evelyn in *Imperial Palace* goes on from strength to strength in his understanding of his life, while the intelligent Gracie chooses to be cherished and seeks joy in a child and in her writing. Only Raingo in *Lord Raingo*, having real sources of content, cannot for long feel it and dies. That the reader is carefully made aware of more glorious might-have-beens does not change the above facts for these people.

Bennett loved mankind. He showed this in every conceivable way in his personal life and he showed it abundantly in his fiction. The fate of common man drew his loving comprehension most of all. And to the common reader he directed most of his prose. Not for him the impressiveness of grandiose obscurity, nor figures more glorious than common clay. Rather, he wanted to honor mankind for their resilience in the daily round.

In looking closely without bias, with a wry humor ever aware of the human absurd, he nevertheless projects a pleased wonder he himself felt and a wonder many of his characters reflect—that they had overcome illusions, chosen and achieved. They do more than merely endure. In his highly organized "synthetic maps" he does not provide a scheme for the cosmos, but that is not because he believed life to be meaningless. Meaning resides in the value of the effort made within the given circumstances. Bennett's pride, confidence, and wonder in common man he declared in a quietly moving statement from his early masterpiece *Anna of the Five Towns*: "The grass grows: though it is not green, it grows. In the very heart of the valley, hedged about with furnaces, a farm still stands, and at harvest-time, the sooty sheaves are gathered" (18). In his imagination the spirit of the sublime joins the candle and the star.

Notes and References

Chapter One

1. Bennett particularly drew upon William Shaw's *When I Was a Child, Recollections of an Old Potter* (London, Methuen, 1903).
2. Thomas Roberts, *Arnold Bennett's Five Towns Origins* (Stoke-on-Trent, 1961).
3. *The Truth About an Author* (London, 1903), p. 25.
4. Margaret Drabble, *Arnold Bennett A Biography* (London, 1974), p. 33.
5. Frederick Marriott, *My Association with Arnold Bennett* (Stoke-on-Trent, 1967).
6. *The Truth About an Author*, p. 27.
7. Ibid., p. 30. The short story and the serial were never published.
8. Dudley Barker, *Writer by Trade* (London, 1966), p. 55.
9. George Sturt (pseudonym George Bourne, 1863–1927) wheelwright and novelist remembered for *The Bettesworth Book* (1901), *Memories of a Surrey Labourer* (1907), and *A Change in the Village* (1911). Their correspondence spread over thirty years.
10. James Hepburn, ed., *Letters of Arnold Bennett, 1889–1915* (London, 1968), 2:12; hereafter cited as Hepburn, *Letters*. I am indebted for many of the biographical details used here to Hepburn's excellent edition of Bennett's letters.
11. This short story is included in *Tales of the Five Towns* (London, 1905).
12. Out of association of the Rhymers' Club, a group of poets, including John Davidson, Lionel Johnson, Ernest Dowson, Arthur Symons, John Todhunter, William Butler Yeats, began *The Yellow Book* to express their discontent with realism and to exhibit their experiments with Impressionism.
13. Hepburn, *Letters*, 2:26-27.
14. See Margaret Drabble's most sympathetic review of what is known about this period in Bennett's life in *Arnold Bennett*, chap. 7.
15. Bennett had taken up calligraphy as a hobby and now felt so sure of the novel he was to write that he wished the completed manuscript to be specially bound and had copies of it holographed for friends.

To view the manuscript is to be astounded at the machine-like perfection of his flow of words.

16. Bennett's writings for the *New Age*, later collected as *Books and Persons: Being Comments on a Past Epoch, 1908–1911* (London, 1917), are not to be confused with articles written under the same title for the *Evening Standard* from 1926 to his death, now collected and edited by Andrew Mylett, entitled: *Arnold Bennett: The 'Evening Standard' Years 'Book and Persons' 1926–1931* (London, 1974).

17. *Saturday Review* (May 8, 1909).

18. She gives tribute to Bennett's care in *A. B. A Minor Marginal Note* (London, 1933).

19. Published volumes of letters to his nephew Richard, to H. G. Wells, to Andre Gide, to J. B. Pinker, represent a small portion of the letters he actually wrote. James Hepburn reports Bennett's secretary, Miss Winnifred Nerney, as saying that Bennett wrote twenty letters a day from 1912 onward.

20. These years are given comprehensive scrutiny in Kinley E. Roby's *A Writer at War: Arnold Bennett 1914–1918* (Baton Rouge, 1972).

21. Barker, *Writer by Trade*, 3 Fame, Chap. 10, "Adopting Richard."

22. Richard Bennett, ed., *Arnold Bennett's Letters to his Nephew* (London, 1936).

23. Dorothy Cheston Bennett, *Arnold Bennett, A Portrait Done At Home* (London, 1935).

24. See Lawrence's letter to Pinker in Hepburn, *Letters*, 1:259-60.

25. See Ezra Pound's portrait of "Mr. Nixon" in "Hugh Selwyn Mauberley," *Selected Poems*, edited with an introduction by T. S. Eliot (London: Faber & Faber, 1933).

26. Virginia Woolf, "Mr. Bennett and Mrs. Brown," *The Hogarth Essays* (London, 1924).

27. After his death a novel fragment called *Dream of Destiny* was published in 1932.

28. Drabble, *Arnold Bennett*, p. 351.

29. "Plot," *Academy* 62 (January-June, 1902):315–16.

30. Edward Wadsworth, *The Black Country* (London: Ovid Press, 1920), p. 1.

31. Ford Madox Ford, *The March of Literature from Confucius to Modern Times* (London: Allen & Unwin, 1939), p. 802.

32. *The Journals of Arnold Bennett, 2, 1911-1921*, ed. Newman Flower (London, 1932), p. 3. *Journal 1* covers 1896-1910. *Journal 3* covers 1921-1928. All references to the *Journals* are to the Newman Flower edition; hereafter cited as *Journals* with appropriate volume number.

33. "Mr. George Gissing. An Enquiry," *Academy* 57 (July-December, 1899):224.
34. *Literary Taste: How to Form It: With Detailed Instruction for Collecting a Complete Library of English* (London, 1909), pp. 12–13; hereafter cited as *Literary Taste*.
35. *The Author's Craft* (London, 1914), p. 18.
36. *Journal 1929* (London, 1930), p. 58. This volume was published separately from the three-volume Newman Flower edition of the *Journals*, and does not have dated entries.
37. *Arnold Bennett and H. G. Wells: A Record of a Personal and Literary Friendship*, ed. Harris Wilson (London, 1960), p. 36; hereafter cited as Wilson, *Bennett and H. G. Wells*.
38. *Literary Taste*, pp. 75-84.
39. James Hepburn, *The Art of Arnold Bennett* (Bloomington, 1963), p. 130.
40. *Literary Taste*, p. 25.
41. "Mr. J. M. Barrie. An Enquiry," *Academy* 59 (July-December 1900):445.
42. *The Author's Craft*, p. 19.
43. Ibid., p. 14.
44. Ibid., p. 24.
45. "Mr. J. M. Barrie. An Enquiry," p. 445.
46. Paul West, *The Modern Novel* (London: Hutchinson, 1963), p. 122.
47. *Literary Taste*, pp. 11–12.
48. "The Author of *Babs the Impossible*," *Academy* 60 (January-June, 1901):347.
49. *Literary Taste*, p. 35.
50. *The Author's Craft*, p. 33.
51. "Comedy or Farce," *Academy* 58 (January-June, 1900);109.
52. *The Author's Craft*, pp. 45–57.

Chapter Two

1. *A Man From the North*, hereafter referred to as *A Man*, was begun in 1895, rewritten and completed in less than a year on May 15, 1896, accepted for publication in the same month by John Lane, but not published until 1898.
2. A part of this novel was thought of in 1894, but Bennett did most of the work on it in 1898, serialized it in 1899 under the title *For Love and Life*, revised it in 1906, and had it first published in book form by Chatto & Windus in 1907.
3. *The Gates of Wrath* was begun in 1899, serialized in 1900, published in book form by Chatto & Windus in 1903.

4. *The Grand Babylon Hotel* was begun in 1900, serialized in 1901, published in book form by Chatto & Windus in 1902.
5. *Anna of the Five Towns*, hereafter referred to as *Anna*, was first drafted in 1896, completed in 1901, and published by Chatto & Windus in 1902.
6. Hepburn, *Letters*, April 24, 1904, 1:49, and May 21, 1904, p. 52.
7. He makes this claim in *How to Become an Author* (London, 1903), pp. 119-20.
8. *Journals*, September 12, 1898, 1:79–80.
9. There is no standard edition of Bennett's work. Where possible I have used first editions throughout this study. All notes cite the edition used. The Bibliography cites first editions. In this case I used *A Man From the North* (London, 1898); hereafter cited as *A Man* with page references to this edition cited in parentheses in the text.
10. Hepburn, *Letters*, 1:139.
11. George Lafourcade, *Arnold Bennett, A Study* (London, 1939), pp. 246–47.
12. *Journals*, 3:52–53.
13. *The Ghost: A Fantasia on Modern Themes* (London, 1907); hereafter referred to as *The Ghost*.
14. *The Gates of Wrath: A Melodrama* (London, 1903); hereafter page references in the text are to this edition.
15. *The Grand Babylon Hotel: A Fantasia on Modern Themes* (London, 1902); hereafter referred to as *The Grand Babylon Hotel*.
16. Wilson, *Bennett and H. G. Wells*, pp. 86–89.
17. *Anna* (London, 1902), p. 4; hereafter page references to this edition are cited in parentheses in the text.
18. Lafourcade, *Arnold Bennett*, pp. 246–47.
19. *The Book of Carlotta*, rev. ed. with new Preface on *Sacred and Profane Love* (New York, 1911), p. vii.
20. Walter Allen, *Arnold Bennett* (London, 1948), p. 53; hereafter cited as Allen, *Bennett*.
21. Vernon Pritchett, *The Living Novel* (London: Chatto & Windus, 1960), p. 134.

Chapter Three

1. Wilson, *Bennett and H. G. Wells*, September 27, 1904, p. 112.
2. Hepburn, *Letters*, December 2, 1903, 1:43, 44 f.
3. Ibid., October 31, 1924, 3:228.
4. *Leonora* (London, 1903), p. 1; hereafter page references to this edition are cited in parentheses in the text.
5. Hepburn, *Letters*, May 25, 1904, 2:189.

6. *Hugo: A Fantasia on Modern Themes* (London, 1906), p. 172; hereafter cited as *Hugo* with page references to this edition cited in parentheses in the text.
7. Preface, *The Book of Carlotta* (New York, 1911). This preface is only included in the American edition under this title. All subsequent references to the novel will be found in the English edition of 1905, entitled *Sacred and Profane Love*.
8. Hepburn, *Letters*, 2:197.
9. "Ouida," pseudonym of Marie Louise de la Ramee (1839–1908). Her novels such as *Strathmore* (1865), *Held in Bondage* (1870), *In Maremma* (1882), *Syrlin* (1890) were probably among those that Bennett said had given him his taste for "liaisons under pink lampshades" as Dudley Barker reports in *Writer by Trade*, p. 39.
10. Bennett told George Sturt that the subject would be "bawdy."
11. Allen, *Bennett*, p. 32.
12. James Hall, *Arnold Bennett: Primitivism and Taste* (Seattle, 1959), p. 46.
13. Hepburn, *Letters*, 1:41.
14. Ibid., 2:239.
15. Ibid.
16. Ibid., p. 235.
17. Ibid., p. 263.
18. Ibid., p. 67 f.
19. Ibid., 1:313 f.
20. *Journals*, May 3, 1906, 1:231.
21. Hepburn, *Letters*, 2:56.
22. This novel was begun April 1, 1905, was completed by May 30 of the same year, and published by Chatto & Windus, 1907.
23. Bennett collaborated with Eden Phillpotts in writing this novel. Phillpotts provided a draft of the plot and Bennett entirely wrote it, beginning January 26, 1906, and finishing April 7, 1907. T. Werner Lauri published the novel later in the year. See Hepburn *Letters*, 1, for Bennett's correspondence on this novel.
24. *Whom God Hath Joined* (London, 1915). All references in the text are to this edition.
25. Hepburn, *Letters*, 1, letter to Alfred Nutt, March 26, 1907, p. 82.
26. Ibid., 2, to Lucie Simpson (February–March, 1907), p. 215.
27. *Journals*, July 22, 1907, 1:238.
28. This novel was written in two months, first published serially as *The Miser's Niece* in *Star*, beginning June 12, 1909; then published by Chapman & Hall in 1910. See Hepburn, *Letters*, 1:91, 96.
29. He had written wholly sympathetic but humorous views of Five

Towns' characters in short stories such as "His Worship the Goose-driver," the first story collected in *Tales of the Five Towns* (London, 1905).

30. Hepburn, *Letters*, September 21, 1907, 1:96.
31. *The Statue* was completed by October 31, 1907, and published by Cassell, March, 1908.
32. Hepburn, *Letters*, 1:93.

Chapter Four

1. The play is a travesty of the novel. See Chap. 8.
2. Five hundred holograph copies of this unique manuscript were published by Wm. Dent in 1927. In the Author's Note prefacing the work, Bennett wrote: "The manuscript here reproduced . . . is, as stated on its title page, the first and last writing . . . : no page, as far as I remember, was destroyed or rewritten." The beautifully bound original is in the Lilly Library, Indiana University, Bloomington, Indiana, U.S.A.
3. Wilson, *Bennett and H. G. Wells*, pp. 150–51.
4. *Buried Alive* has continuously been popular after some initial indifference. The play version, *The Great Adventure*, was very successful, the film called *Holy Matrimony* was equally so, and in 1967 it was turned into a Broadway musical called *Darling of the Day*, starring Vincent Price and Patricia Routledge.
5. Bennett used these words to describe George Moore's accomplishments in *A Mummer's Wife* in *Fame and Fiction, An Enquiry into Certain Popularities* (London, 1901), p. 257. It describes Bennett's feat as well.
6. *The Old Wives' Tale* (London, 1908), p. 4; hereafter all page references cited in the text are from this edition.
7. E. K. Brown, *Rhythm in the Novel* (U.S.A., 1963), pp. 16–18.
8. Hepburn, *Art of Arnold Bennett*, pp. 55–65.
9. Walter Allen, *The English Novel*, p. 309.

Chapter Five

1. However, the younger writers, Woolf, Lawrence, were particularly harsh in their published views of Bennett's writing. They would not have been willing to recognize any influence upon them from that quarter.
2. *Journals, 1896–1910*, 1:291.
3. Hepburn, *Letters*, 1:102 f,; 2:227 f.
4. Ibid., 2:230.

5. *The Glimpse: An Adventure of the Soul* (London: Chapman & Hall, 1912), p. 308.
6. *Journals, 1911–1921*, 2:67.
7. John Lucas, *Arnold Bennett: A Study of His Fiction* (London, 1974), p. 145.
8. *Clayhanger* (London: Methuen, 1910), p. 3; hereafter page references cited in the text are to this edition.
9. Lucas, *Arnold Bennett*, p. 145.
10. *Hilda Lessways* (London: Methuen, 1961), p. 17; hereafter page references cited in the text are to this edition.
11. *Journals, 1896–1910*, 2:386.
12. *Journals*, 1:313.
13. *The Card* (London: Methuen, 38th ed. [reset], reprinted 1965), p. 242.
14. Hepburn, *Letters*, 1:119–20.
15. Ibid., p. 315n.
16. Ibid., 2:311.
17. *These Twain* (London: Methuen, 1962). All page references cited in the text are to this edition.

Chapter Six

1. *Journals, 1911–1921*, 1:128.
2. Kinley E. Roby, *A Writer at War*, p. 93.
3. Lucas, *Arnold Bennett*, p. 174.
4. Drabble, *Arnold Bennett*, p. 214.
5. Hepburn, *Letters*, 1:228–29.
6. Ibid., p. 159.
7. *Journals, 1911–1921*, 2:198.
8. Ibid., p. 289.
9. Ibid., p. 227.
10. Ibid., p. 196.
11. Ibid., pp. 232–33.
12. *Riceyman Steps* (London, 1923), p. 1. All further references given in the text are to this edition.
13. Hepburn, *Letters*, 3:210.

Chapter Seven

1. *Lord Raingo* (London: Cassell & Co., Pocket Library Edition, 1928), p. 1. All subsequent references in the text are to this edition.
2. Kinley E. Roby, *A Writer at War*, pp. 277, 281.
3. Hepburn, *Letters*, 1:282.

4. *Journals, 1921–1928*, 3:140.
5. Ibid., p. 168.
6. *Accident* (London: Cassell & Co., 1929), p. 54.
7. Hepburn, *Letters*, 3:339.
8. Ibid., p. 345.
9. Ibid., p. 346 f.
10. *Imperial Palace* (London, 1930), p. 17. All subsequent references in the text are to this edition.
11. Hepburn, *Letters*, 1:407.

Chapter Eight

1. This volume has been republished with *The Grim Smile of the Five Towns* by Chatto & Windus, 1964.
2. *The Grim Smile of the Five Towns* (London, 1907). Edition used: Phoenix Library, 1928, p. 210; subsequent page references in the text are to this edition.
3. Hepburn, *Letters*, 2:289.
4. *Don Juan de Marana: A Play in Four Acts* (London, 1923), pp. xiii–xviii. A private printing.
5. *Journals, 1921–1928*, October 19, 1927, 3:239.
6. *The Snake Charmer*, in *One-Act Plays for Stage and Study*, Sixth Series, (London: Samuel French, 1934).
7. *Piccadilly*, in *The Collected Works of Arnold Bennett*, (New York: Books for Libraries Press, 1975).
8. Hepburn, *Letters*, 3:320.
9. Ibid., 1:389.
10. These articles are collected in Andrew Mylett, ed., *Arnold Bennett The 'Evening Standard' Years*.
11. Hepburn, *Letters*, 1:278.
12. Mylett, *The 'Evening Standard' Years*, p. 345.
13. *The Truth About an Author* (London: Methuen, 1928), p. vii.

Selected Bibliography

There is no standard edition of Bennett's work. The Primary Sources lists first editions. The Secondary Sources lists the editions used.

PRIMARY SOURCES

1. Novels

Accident. London: Cassell, 1929; New York: Doran, 1928. Serialized as "Train de luxe" in the *Daily Express* from July 16, 1928.

Anna of the Five Towns: A Novel. London: Chatto & Windus, 1902. Dramatized as *Cupid and Commonsense*, 1909.

Buried Alive: A Tale of These Days. London: Chapman & Hall, 1908. Dramatized as *The Great Adventure*, 1913.

The Card: A Story of Adventure in the Five Towns. London: Methuen, 1911. Serialized in *The Times Weekly* from February 4, 1910. Published as *Denry the Audacious.* New York: Dutton, 1911.

The City of Pleasure: A Fantasia on Modern Themes. London: Chatto & Windus, 1907. Serialized in *The Staffordshire Sentinel* from January 6, 1906.

Clayhanger. London: Methuen, 1910.

Dream of Destiny: A Unfinished Novel. London: Cassell, 1932.

The Gates of Wrath: A Melodrama. London: Chatto & Windus, 1903.

The Ghost: A Fantasia on Modern Themes. London: Chatto & Windus, 1907.

The Glimpse: An Adventure of the Soul. London: Chapman & Hall, 1909; New York: D. Appleton & Co., 1909.

The Grand Babylon Hotel: A Fantasia on Modern Themes. London: Chatto & Windus, 1902. Serialized in *The Golden Penny* from February 2, 1901. Published as *T. Racksole and Daughter.* New York: New Amsterdam Book Co., 1902.

A Great Man: A Frolic. London: Chatto & Windus, 1904.

Helen with the High Hand: An Idyllic Diversion. London: Chapman & Hall,

1910. Serialized as "The Miser's Niece" in *The Star* from June 12, 1909. It was dramatized by Richard Pryce in 1914.

Hilda Lessways. London: Methuen, 1911; New York: Dutton, 1911.

Hugo: A Fantasia on Modern Themes. London: Chatto & Windus, 1906. Serialized in *Today* from May 3, 1905.

Imperial Palace. London: Cassell, 1930.

Leonora: A Novel. London: Chatto & Windus, 1903.

Lilian. London: Cassell, 1922.

The Lion's Share. London: Cassell, 1916. Serialized in the *Metropolitan Magazine* from October, 1915.

Lord Raingo. London: Cassell, 1926; New York: Doran 1926. Serialized in the *Evening Standard* September 20, 1926.

A Man From the North. London & New York: John Lane, 1898.

Mr. Prohack. London: Methuen, 1922. Serialized in *The Delineator* from July, 1921 and in *The Westminster Gazette* from November 7, 1921. Dramatized in collaboration with E. Knoblock, 1927.

The Old Wives' Tale: A Novel. London: Chapman & Hall, 1908. With Preface, New York: Doran, 1911.

The Pretty Lady: A Novel. London: Cassell, 1918.

The Price of Love: A Tale. London: Methuen, 1914; New York: Harper & Bros., 1914. Serialized in *Harper's Magazine* from December, 1913.

The Regent: A Five Towns Story of Adventure in London. London: Methuen, 1913. *"The Old Adam": A Story of Adventure.* New York: Doran, 1913. Serialized in *London Magazine* from November, 1912.

Riceyman Steps: A Novel. London: Cassell, 1923.

The Roll-Call. London: Hutchinson, 1918.

Sacred and Profane Love: A Novel in Three Episodes. London: Chatto & Windus, 1905. *The Book of Carlotta.* New York: Doran, 1911. Dramatized in 1919.

The Sinews of War: A Romance of London and the Sea. In collaboration with Eden Phillpotts. London: T. Werner Laurie, 1906. Serialized in *T. P.'s Weekly* from March 2, 1906.

The Statue. In collaboration with Eden Phillpotts. London: Cassell, 1908; New York: Moffat Yard, 1908.

The Strange Vanguard: A Fantasia. London: Cassell, 1928; New York: Doran, 1927.

Teresa of Watling Street: A Fantasia on Modern Themes. London: Chatto & Windus, 1904.

These Twain. London: Methuen, 1916; New York: Doran, 1915.

Venus Rising From the Sea. London: Cassell, 1931.

Whom God Hath Joined. London: David Nutt, 1906.

2. Collected Editions of Short Stories

Elsie and the Child: A Tale of Riceyman Steps and Other Stories. London: Cassell, 1924. (13 stories)

The Grim Smile of the Five Towns. London: Chapman & Hall, 1907. (13 stories)

The Loot of Cities: Being the Adventures of a Millionaire in Search of Joy. London: Alston Rivers, 1905. (6 related stories)

The Matador of the Five Towns and Other Stories. London: Methuen, 1912. (22 stories)

The Night Visitor and Other Stories. London: Cassell, 1931. (17 stories)

Short Stories of Today and Yesterday. London: George C. Harrop, 1928. (10 stories from previous editions)

Tales of the Five Towns. London: Chatto & Windus, 1905. (13 stories)

The Woman Who Stole Everything and Other Stories. London: Cassell, 1927. (13 stories)

3. Plays

Body and Soul: A Play in Four Acts. London: Chatto & Windus, 1920.

The Bright Island. London: Golden Cockerel Press, 1924.

Cupid and Commonsense: A Play in Four Acts, with a Preface on the Crisis in the Theatre. London: New Age Press, 1909. Adapted from *Anna of the Five Towns.*

Don Juan de Marana: A Play in Four Acts. London: T. Werner Laurie, 1923. Privately printed for subscribers.

Flora. London: Rich & Cowan, 1933. Published in *Five Three Act Plays.*

A Good Woman: A Farce in One Act. London: Gowans & Gray, 1900. Published in *Polite Farces for the Drawing Room.*

The Great Adventure: A Play of Fancy in Four Acts. London: Methuen, 1913. Adapted from *Buried Alive.*

The Honeymoon: A Comedy in Three Acts. London: Methuen, 1911.

Ides of March. In collaboration with Fred Alcock. New York: Samuel French, 1934. Published in *One-Act Plays for Stage and Study, Eighth Series: Twenty Contemporary Plays by American English and Japanese Writers.*

Judith: A Play in Three Acts, Founded on the Apocryphal Book of "Judith." London: Chatto & Windus, 1919.

London Life: A Play in Three Acts and Nine Scenes. In collaboration with E. Knoblock. London: Chatto & Windus, 1924.

The Love Match: A Play in Five Scenes. London: Chatto & Windus, 1922.

Milestones: A Play in Three Acts. In collaboration with E. Knoblauch. London: Methuen, 1912.

Mr. Prohack: A Comedy in Three Acts. In collaboration with E. Knoblock. London: Chatto & Windus, 1927.

A Question of Sex: A Farce in One Act. London: Gowans & Gray, 1900.
Published in *Polite Farces for the Drawing Room.*
*Sacred and Profane Love: A Play in Four Acts Founded upon the Novel of the
Same Name.* London: Chatto & Windus, 1919.
The Snake Charmer. London: Rich & Cowan, 1933.
The Stepmother: A Farce in One Act. London: Gowans & Gray, 1900.
Published in *Polite Farces for the Drawing Room.*
The Title: A Comedy in Three Acts. London: Chatto & Windus, 1918.
What the Public Wants: A Play in Four Acts. London: Duckworth,
1909.

4.   Film Scenario
"Piccadilly": Story of the Film. London: Readers Library Publishing Co.,
1929.

5.   Operas
Judith: An Opera in One Act. Libretto by Arnold Bennett. Music by
Eugene Goossens. London: J. & W. Chester, 1935.
Don Juan de Marana: Opera in Four Acts. Libretto by Arnold
Bennett. Music by Eugene Goossens. London: J. & W. Chester
(1935).
Rosalys: A Music Play for Girls in Two Acts. Libretto by E. Arnold Bennett.
Music by James Brown. Libretto published in Margaret Locherbie-
Goff, *La Jeunesse d'Arnold Bennett (1867–1904).* Avesne-sur-Aelpe,
France: Editions de l'Observateur, n.d.

6.   Literary Criticism
*Arnold Bennett: The 'Evening Standard' Years 'Books and Persons' 1926–
1931.* Edited by Andrew Mylett. London: Chatto & Windus,
1974.
The Author's Craft. London: Hodder & Stoughton, 1914; New York:
Doran, 1914.
Books and Persons: Being Comments on a Past Epoch, 1908–1911. London:
Chatto & Windus, 1917.
Fame and Fiction: An Enquiry into Certain Popularities. London: Grant
Richards, 1901.
How to Become an Author: A Practical Guide. London: C. Arthur Pearson,
1903.
Journalism for Women: A Practical Guide. London: John Lane, The Bodley
Head, 1898.
*Literary Taste: How to Form It: With Detailed Instruction for Collecting a
Complete Library of English.* London: New Age Press, 1909.
The Truth About an Author. London: Archibald & Constable & Co., 1903.

7. Pocket Philosophies
The Feast of St. Friend. London: Hodder & Stoughton, 1911.
How to Live on Twenty-Four Hours a Day. London: New Age Press, 1908.
How to Make the Best of Life. London: Hodder & Stoughton, 1923.
The Human Machine. London: New Age Press, 1908.
Mental Efficiency and Other Hints to Men and Women. London: Hodder & Stoughton, 1912.
Our Women: Chapters on the Sex-Discord. London: Cassell, 1920.
The Plain Man and His Wife. London: Hodder & Stoughton, 1913.
The Reasonable Life: Being Hints for Men and Women. London: A. C. Fifield, 1907.
Self and Self-Management. London: Hodder & Stoughton, 1918.

8. Essays, Pamphlets, Travel
From the Log of the Velsa. New York: Century Company, 1914.
Liberty: A Statement of the British Case. London: Hodder & Stoughton, 1914.
Mediterranean Scenes. Rome-Greece-Constantinople. London: Cassell, 1928.
A National Responsibility: Future Employment of the Disabled. Manchester and London: John Heywood, 1917.
Over There: War Scenes on the Western Front. London: Methuen, 1915.
Paris Nights and Other Impressions of Places and People. London: Hodder & Stoughton, 1913; New York: Doran, 1913.
The Religious Interregnum. London: Ernest Benn, 1929.
The Savour of Life: Essays in Gusto. London: Cassell, 1928.
Things That Have Interested Me. London: Chatto & Windus, 1921.
Things That Have Interested Me. Second Series. London: Chatto & Windus, 1923.
Things That Have Interested Me. Third Series. London: Chatto & Windus, 1923.
Those United States. London: Martin Secker, 1912.

9. Letters
Arnold Bennett's Letters to His Nephew. Edited by Richard Bennett. Preface by Frank Swinnerton. London: Heinemann, 1936; New York: Harper & Bros., 1935.
Arnold Bennett in Love. Arnold Bennett and his Wife Marguerite Soulië A Correspondence. Edited and translated by George and Jean Beardmore. London: David Bruce & Watson, 1972.
Arnold Bennett and H.G. Wells: A Record of A Personal and a Literary Friendship. Edited by Harris Wilson. London: Rupert Hart-Davis, 1960.
Correspondence Andre Gide—Arnold Bennett: Vingt Ans d'Amitie Litteraire

(1911–1931). Introduction and Notes by Linette F. Brugmans. Geneva: Droz Library, 1964.
Letters of Arnold Bennett. Edited by James Hepburn. Vol. 1. *Letters to J.B. Pinker*. London: Oxford University Press, 1966; Vol. 2 *1889–1915*. London: Oxford University Press, 1968; Vol. 3 *1916–1931*. London: Oxford University Press, 1970.

10.   Other Works including Previously Unpublished Bennett Letters
Bennett, Dorothy Cheston. *Arnold Bennett: A Portrait Done at Home, Together With 170 Letters from A.B.* London: Jonathan Cape, 1935.
Hart-Davis, Rupert. *Hugh Walpole: A Biography*. London: Macmillan, 1952.
Jean-Aubry, G. *Twenty Letters to Conrad*. London: First Edition Club, 1926.
Pound, Reginald. *Arnold Bennett: A Biography*. London: Heinemann, 1952.

11.   Journals
Florentine Journal 1st April–25th May 1910. Illustrated by the author, with introduction by Sacheverell Sitwell. London: Chatto & Windus, 1967.
Journal 1929. London: Cassell, 1930. *Journal of Things New and Old*. New York: Doubleday Doran, 1930.
The Journals of Arnold Bennett, 1896–1910. The Journals of Arnold Bennett, 1911–1921. The Journals of Arnold Bennett, 1921–1928. Edited by Newman Flower. London: Cassell, 1932.
The Journals. Edited by Frank Swinnerton. First publication of the missing volume six. London: Penguin, 1971.

12.   Autobiography
Sketches for Autobiography. Edited with introduction by James Hepburn. London: George Allen & Unwin, 1979.

SECONDARY SOURCES

Allen, Walter. *Arnold Bennett*. London: Home & Van Thal, 1948. Concludes that Bennett is not more than a minor master who produced some solid and satisfying novels.
Barker, Dudley. *Writer by Trade, a View of Arnold Bennett*. London: Allen

& Unwin, 1966. A lively portrait drawing upon some hitherto unpublished material, but not appreciably different in assessment from Reginald Pound's earlier biography.

Bennett, Dorothy Cheston. *Arnold Bennett A Portrait Done at Home Together With 170 Letters from A.B.* New York: Claude Kendall and Willoughby Sharp, 1935. A limited view of Bennett in love in his last eight years.

Bennett, Marguerite. *Arnold Bennett.* London: A.M. Philpott, 1925. The view of Bennett's wife vainly trying to accommodate herself to the circumstances of her marriage.

Darton, F.J. Harvey. *Arnold Bennett.* London: Nisbet & Co., n.d. A brief provocative assessment of Bennett's career to the 1920s published in Bennett's lifetime.

Drabble, Margaret. *Arnold Bennett a Biography.* London: Weidenfeld & Nicholson, 1974. A richly detailed, sensitive critical biography.

Hall, James. *Arnold Bennett: Primitivism and Taste.* Seattle: University of Washington Press, 1959. With some forcing of fact to fit theory, this is, nevertheless, an interesting exploration of Bennett's work as an attempt to realize some middle ground between the values inherent in primitivism and values perceived in more aristocratic traditions.

Hepburn, James. *The Art of Arnold Bennett.* Bloomington: Indiana University Press, 1963. Sees Bennett as a psychological portraitist of considerable penetration, a sophisticated and systematic symbolist.

Johnson, L.G. *Arnold Bennett of the Five Towns.* London: C.W. Daniel Co. 1924. Concentrates upon five of the Five Towns novels to demonstrate the author's view of the nature of Bennett's intellect and imagination.

Lafourcade, Georges. *Arnold Bennett, A Study.* London: Frederick Muller, 1939. The first comprehensive study of Bennett's varied forms of writing. Concludes that Bennett forms significant link between the Victorians and the Moderns.

Lucas, John. *Arnold Bennett A Study of His Fiction.* London: Methuen, 1974. Gives interesting new readings of some of the novels. Judges Bennett deserves more praise.

Marriott, Frederick. *My Association with Arnold Bennett.* Stoke-on-Trent: Keele University Library Occasional Publications 3, 1967. Warm recollections of an art teacher who appreciated Bennett's varied talents in music and art and admired his talent for friendship.

Miller, Anita. *Arnold Bennett An Annotated Bibliography 1887–1932.* New York and London: Garland Publishing, 1977. An invaluable bibliographical tool.

Pound, Reginald. *Arnold Bennett A Biography.* London: Heinemann,

1952. The first full portrait. Generally appreciative of Bennett as artist, but more interested in Bennett as social "card."

Roberts, Thomas R. *Arnold Bennett's Five Towns Origins.* Stoke-on-Trent: Libraries, Museums and Information Committee, 1961. A detailed brochure of Bennett's ancestry, education, and early life.

Roby, Kinley E. *A Writer at War: Arnold Bennett, 1914–1918.* Baton Rouge: Louisiana State University Press, 1972. Maintains that Bennett's experiences during the war stimulated him out of an abyss of creative sterility. Gives interesting reassessments of Bennett's postwar fiction.

Simon, J.B. *Arnold Bennett and His Novels.* Oxford: Basil Blackwell, 1936. A somewhat rambling account giving mainly synopses of Bennett's work.

Smith, Pauline. *A.B. A Minor Marginal Note.* London: Jonathan Cape, 1933. A loving remembrance by a sensitive, appreciative protégée.

Swinnerton, Frank. *Arnold Bennett A Last Word.* New York: Doubleday & Co., 1978. A brief reminiscence of Bennett, emphasizing his lovableness and the personal difficulties of his last years.

Wain, John. *Arnold Bennett.* New York: Columbia University Press, 1967. Reaffirms the view of Bennett as the first and only English novelist to cultivate determinedly Continental Realism. Bennett's "objectivity" minus the "religious impulse" places his novels below the rank of world masterpieces, Wain claims.

West, Geoffrey. *The Problem of Arnold Bennett.* London: Joiner & Steele, 1933. Sees a seriously divided Bennett who in the end had sacrificed artistic integrity to journalistic facility.

West, Rebecca. *Arnold Bennett Himself.* New York: John Day, 1931. Claims the man was more remarkable than his work, but makes the interesting statement that "Bennett stood for a purer liberation . . . for the establishment of democracy among the perceptions."

Woolf, Virginia. "Mr. Bennett and Mrs. Brown." In *The Hogarth Essays.* London: Hogarth Press, 1924. A counterattack presenting Bennett as a purveyor of useless detail in fiction.

Wright, Walter. *Arnold Bennett: Romantic Realist.* Lincoln: University of Nebraska Press, 1971. Surveys Bennett's writings to show that Bennett early moved away from objective realism-naturalism to emphasize compassionate presentation.

Index